How to Assess your IT Investment

For Ailsa, Christine and David

How to Assess your IT Investment

A study of methods and practice

Barbara Farbey, Frank Land and David Targett

Published in association with
Management Today

Butterworth-Heinemann Ltd
Linacre House, Jordan Hill, Oxford OX2 8DP

 PART OF REED INTERNATIONAL BOOKS

OXFORD   LONDON   BOSTON
MUNICH   NEW DELHI   SINGAPORE   SYDNEY
TOKYO   TORONTO   WELLINGTON

First published 1993

British Library Cataloguing in Publication Data
Farbey, Barbara
    How to Assess your IT Investment: A study
    of methods and practice
    I. Title
    658.4038

ISBN 0 7506 0654 1

Composition by Genesis Typesetting, Laser Quay, Rochester, Kent
Printed and bound in Great Britain by Redwood Press, Melksham, Wiltshire

Contents

Preface

> Everybody does cost/benefit analysis on projects. Most of them are
> fictional. The saddest part is that it is not just the benefits that are
> fictional, but the costs are as well. They don't begin to assess what the real
> costs of the system are. You do cost/benefit analysis to get money.
>
> We have trouble convincing ourselves of value in business terms. We
> cost justify new systems on the basis of lies, and having justified [them] on
> the basis of lies and overstatement, we then don't measure the true
> business value.[1]

These despairing words present a challenge to the information systems
community and to a book such as this. A critique so formidable and well
founded requires an answer if we are not to give in to the partisanship,
bias and irrationality which the above extract so clearly implies. We
have to show not only that evaluation can be carried out honestly, but
that by doing so the organization will achieve something of value.

We believe that such evaluation is possible and that it is worthwhile.
At the same time we believe that this is true only when it is seen for what
it is: a human endeavour to find agreement on the worth of a social
action, not a method of pinning numbers on things to prove or disprove
a case. We are also convinced that progress will be made only by
explicitly acknowledging the human and fallible aspects of evaluation
and facing them squarely. Driving the cut and thrust of organizational
life underground to achieve a tidy, 'scientific' result will not do. There
can be reason, and good science, in evaluation, but only if the voices of
unreason and pseudo-science are brought into the open, examined and
stilled. In this book we address some of the major issues associated with
the evaluation of information systems. Some of these issues are as old as
IT itself. Others are new – consequences of the technology, the
organizations and the concerns of the 1990s. Characteristically, many of
the issues surrounding the newer applications of IT are those of
alignment. Aligning evaluation and strategy has always been important.
In the face of today's escalating budgets it is crucial.

Many of the insights and much of the data on which this book is based
are derived from a research project carried out by the authors in the late
1980s. The research was sponsored by a major supplier of IT equipment
and the study was based on an investigation of 16 projects in

organizations who were using the research sponsor's systems. As a vendor, the company needed to know how its clients (and potential clients) evaluated the systems marketed by the company, how the purchase of the system was justified and whether the outcomes of successful sales yielded the net benefits the clients had expected. We refer to the cases throughout the book. They are not a statistical sample, but they were collected in pairs from different industries. The companies were also willing collaborators.

From these cases and others we provide examples of how organizations carry out evaluations and indicate the problems faced by the evaluator. We review many of the methods and techniques used. Finally, we suggest how an evaluator might choose the most suitable evaluation tools for the organization.

Plan of the book

Part One (Chapters 1–3) describes the challenges which face the evaluator. The chapters sketch in the background and context of evaluation. Chapter 1 describes evaluation in the context of the changing role of IT. Chapter 2 considers why evaluation is important and why it is a problem. It goes on to list the stages in the lifetime of a project when evaluation is carried out and how the purposes of evaluation change with the timing. Chapter 3 deals with the foundations of evaluation, the great benefit hunt. It presents a comprehensive categorization and listing of the business benefits which the organization hopes to receive from its financial investment in IT. The chapter then reviews the categories of costs which the decision to invest will generate.

Part Two (Chapters 4–5) reports on current practice. Chapter 4 describes the research project which showed how, in the companies we investigated, 16 projects were evaluated. Chapter 5 presents several of the cases studied in the research in more detail. They illustrate the practical problems involved in evaluation and show that evaluation is inextricably linked to a series of other management issues.

Part Three (Chapters 6–8) sets out some of the options faced in terms of methods and techniques available to the evaluator. Chapter 6 reports on some of the findings of the writers, consultants and researchers who have investigated the problem of evaluation in a variety of contexts. Chapters 7 and 8 review and analyse some of the more interesting evaluation methods used in practice or advocated in the literature. Chapter 7 focuses on methods which attempt to provide numerical measures of cost and benefit in order to support comparisons of one project with another and to help make the investment decision. Chapter 8 emphasizes methods which are meant to explore the potential value of systems, taking into account the viewpoints of a variety of stake-holders.[2]

Part Four (Chapters 9–12) demonstrates a new approach to classifying information systems and to helping evaluators choose an appropriate mix of evaluation approaches and tools. Chapter 9 classifies the characteristics of information systems applications and projects in a way which helps to identify suitable evaluation methods. Chapter 10 identifies the factors which are most relevant to the choice of evaluation method. Chapter 11 sets out a new approach whose objective is to enable the evaluator to match the investment situation with an appropriate evaluation method. Chapter 12 sets out our concluding thoughts.

Summary

The objective of the book is to demonstrate that IT evaluation faces many problems, but that it need not be treated merely as an exercise in game-playing. It is possible to add real value to the organization by choosing to deal with the problems openly and choosing an appropriate method. IT evaluation has to be aligned with strategic IT thinking.

Notes and references

1 The MIT research project 'Management in the 1990s' was a collaborative project between 12 major global corporations from North America and the UK. One of the research reports stemming from the study looked at information system assessment. The quotation is taken from: Wilson, D. D. (1988) *Assessing IT Performance: What the Experts Say*, Management in the 1990s Working Paper 88-050, MIT, Boston, Mass.
2 The term 'stakeholder' denotes any individual or group of individuals who are affected directly or indirectly by the introduction of a new system. The term was introduced by Russell Ackoff in the context of evaluating organizational change.

Barbara Farbey
Frank Land
David Targett

Part One

Part One (Chapters 1–3) describes the challenges which face the evaluator. The chapters sketch in the background and context of evaluation.

- **Chapter 1** describes evaluation in the context of the changing role of information technology.
- **Chapter 2** considers why evaluation is important and why it is a problem. It goes on to list the stages in the lifetime of a project when evaluation is carried out and how the purposes of evaluation change with the timing.
- **Chapter 3** deals with the foundations of evaluation, the great benefit hunt. It presents a comprehensive categorization and listing of the business benefits which the organization hopes to receive from its financial investment in IT. The chapter then reviews the categories of costs which the decision to invest will generate.

1 Information technology: the role of evaluation

Introduction – the changing role of information technology

The role of IT in all types of organization has changed. In consequence management methods are having to change and that is why this book has been written.

An old problem?

The problems of evaluating and justifying investments in the use of IT are not new. For the past three decades managers have expressed concerns about the value they are getting from IT investments, and for the past three decades they have been searching for an ideal way of solving the problems.

In 1961 IFIP (International Federation for Information Processing) held its first conference on the Economics of Informatics, and published the outcome in a book with the same title.[1]

In 1971 the NCC (National Computing Council) commissioned a survey of how investments in IT were justified by British industry and commerce.[2] This was followed by a conference which discussed alternative approaches to the problem.

In 1974 IFIP held its second conference on the Economics of Informatics and again published the proceedings as a book.[3]

In 1976 EDUCOM, an American educational consultancy, held a conference entitled 'We can produce cost effective systems now' which surveyed methods of evaluation.[4]

In 1987 IFIP convened yet another conference on Information Systems Assessment, and published the proceedings under the same title.[5]

When asked by the House of Commons Select Committee on Trade and Industry in 1988 what issue the government needed to address most urgently in relation to IT, Tony Cleaver, Chief Executive of IBM UK, suggested finding reliable ways of assessing investment in information systems. The government responded by commissioning a report on IT evaluation for small and medium-sized companies.

Various studies throughout the 1980s and into the 1990s have investigated what IT and general management felt to be the critical issues relating to IT which were causing them concern. The problem of finding convincing methods of justifying expenditure on information systems appeared high on or even top of the list.

It is clear that the problem of justification has continued to worry executives for many years. Indeed, the results of the 1972 NCC survey show that business practice and business concerns with respect to the problem were not very different from those of today. The argument about achieving effective use rather than merely efficient use was equally present in the early 1970s. The opportunities and the language have changed in that concerns about competitive advantage and the strategic use of IT now dominate the discussions in the boardroom.

A new problem?

Since the mid-1980s the understanding of what IT is has changed for two reasons, as illustrated in Figure 1.1. First, there have been rapid advances in the capabilities of IT, such as increased power and improved linkages and connectivity, combined with substantial reductions in its cost. If cars had improved in price at the same rate as IT, an upmarket model could now be purchased for the price of a bus ticket into town. Whether there would be any road space to drive it on is another matter.

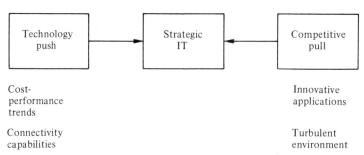

Figure 1.1 Why IT's role has changed

Second, organizations in both public and private sectors have been subject to severe competitive pressures and turbulence in their spheres of operation. The MIT90s research programme[6] described these pressures as organizational turbulence and highlighted four aspects of the changes affecting organizations:

- *Social*: consumers' heightened expectations of quality and price, environmental issues.

- *Political*: collapse of the USSR, opportunities in Eastern Europe, regulatory changes.
- *Economic*: US trade and budget deficits, rise of Japan, implications of a united Germany.
- *Technological*: rapid developments in product, process and information technology, advances in the biosciences.

These same pressures are also affecting the way organizations are structured and the roles people are expected to play in them.

As a result of technology push and competitive pull, IT now does more than automate support processes. More than just supporting functional processes, it is increasingly being applied to the cores of businesses; more than just automating, it is transforming industries, organizations, business processes and management methods.

'Core' is difficult to define but examples are plentiful. Retailers' use of electronic point of sales (EPOS) systems and travel agents' use of computerized booking systems are just two examples of information systems which operate at the core of the business and which have transformed the way business is carried out. Developments such as credit cards, depending upon IT for the growth in their use, have added new dimensions and totally new businesses to computer-based organizational activities.

When applied in this way IT gives benefits much wider than cost and manpower reductions. These benefits sometimes amount to competitive advantage. The case studies describing such achievements are well known: American Airlines, Baxter Hospital Supplies, McKesson, Otis Elevators and many others.

IT has also had the effect of seeming to shorten geographical distances and enabling organizations to cross international boundaries. Just as the development a century ago of telegraph and telephone allowed local companies to become national companies, so modern information systems improve communications within an organization and promote close alliances between organizations. A European car manufacturer can be linked more closely with offices and agents on other continents. It can communicate electronically with suppliers in other European countries and information systems help it to establish joint ventures with other manufacturers. As a result international trade in several industries has been transformed.

Just as IT investments are of a different scope, organizations' IT concerns are no longer just the cost of and the time to deliver projects. They are now whether their IT investments are gaining them short-term competitive advantage, whether further investments can maintain their lead, and whether their competitors' investments are putting them at a competitive disadvantage.

Of course it would be wrong to suggest that IT investments always, or even mostly, lead to success. Nor is it to be expected that businesses which are not competitive will become so purely as a result of an IT investment.

For a variety of reasons, there have been many disasters but they tend not to be well publicized. Other organizations fall between success and disaster, and many do not know whether they have been successful or not. In some industries it is necessary to spend vast amounts on information systems . . . or cease to compete. Banking is an example. In spite of the large information system expenditures there is no competitive advantage, just competitive disadvantage if you fail to spend or spend wrongly. This uncertainty and unpredictability points to the need for improved evaluation.

The changing role of IT is summarized in Figure 1.2.

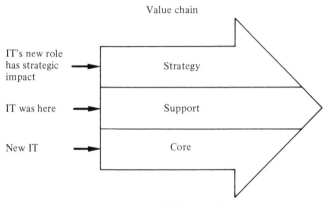

Figure 1.2 IT's new role

The changing role of managers

'The international division of labour' is only a fancy way of describing what people do when they go to work . . . technology has had by far the greatest impact . . .[7]

In the 1960s the general management perspective on computer operations was that they were a technical matter. The general management role was to check whether projects were on time and under budget, or not. This role did not appear to require general managers to know much, if anything, about computers. In practice this was a mistaken view.

The situation now is very different. There are four inescapable reasons why senior general managers today need to be even more closely involved with IT:

- *IT affects strategic issues*. If IT can gain, or lose, competitive advantage and if it can radically alter market share, then a chief executive can hardly regard it as a technical matter only. A pharmaceutical company dramatically increased market share when it put computers linked to an information system about its products on doctors' desks.
- *IT is at the core of business processes*. Many organizations could no longer function without IT. A bank which did not offer the customer services that computerization brings would have a poor future. Some business processes have been changed radically by IT, e.g. the buying and selling of shares.
- *IT accounts for large expenditures*. In many organizations IT expenditure regularly runs at 4% of revenue or more. For some banks it is as high as 10%. A recent survey revealed that 50% of new capital expenditure is on IT.
- *IT is complex*. It needs to be managed across functional and organizational boundaries. Only senior management can do this.

Even if the strategic and management arguments are ignored it is certain that a chief executive will pay close attention to major expenditures. For some the IT revolution has not yet occurred but they have seen how quickly it has struck elsewhere and do not want to be left behind by competitors. Whatever the reasons, IT is firmly on the general management agenda. This includes a need to be more concerned with evaluation.

The changing range of benefits

At the heart of IT's new role is the wider range of benefits IT can now bring. Traditional IT applications reduce costs but this does not transform business processes, inter-organizational networks and business scope. Increased efficiency can bring strategic advantage, e.g. by reducing price, but it is likely to be marginal and transitory. Besides efficiency, IT has the potential to provide wide benefits, including:

- *Competitive advantage*: e.g. increasing bargaining power in the competitive arena, creating barriers to entry, tying in customers.
- *Co-operative advantage*: strategic alliances based on IT.
- *Diversification*: widening business scope, offering new products.
- *Marketing*: improving customer service, targeting marketing, adding value to products.

- *Effective management*: improving delivery information, getting new products to market faster, providing a just-in-time service.

These are just some of the wider benefits IT now provides and many writers have tried to describe them and their development over the years in different and imaginative ways. For example, the Index Group use the matrix in Figure 1.3 which shows IT impacting at the level of the individual, the function and the whole organization. It shows benefits of efficiency, effectiveness and transformation. The development of IT

AREA OF IMPACT

	Individual	Function	Organization
Efficiency	**Era II** Task mechanization e.g. word processing	**Era I** Process automation e.g. payroll	**Era III** Boundary extension e.g. virtual orgs
Effectiveness	Work improvement e.g. d-top publishing	Functional enhancement e.g. inventory info	Service enhancement e.g. booking systems
Transformation	Role expansion e.g. co-ordination roles	Functional redefinition e.g. sales/stock links	Product innovation e.g. selling info

BENEFITS

Figure 1.3 The matrix of benefits and their impact

applications is described as falling into three eras. The matrix is not intended to suggest that organizations move through it one box at a time. An organization is likely to be operating in several boxes at once and there is no prescribed route for moving through the matrix.

- *Era I*. IT was first applied to functional areas, bringing efficiency and, later, effectiveness benefits: automating the payroll reduced staff costs; automating stock control provided better information on stockouts and deliveries.
- *Era II*. Next came the application of IT to the individual with the advent of microcomputers. For example, word-processing brought improvements to office workers.
- *Era III*. The present has seen IT bringing about transformations and affecting the whole organization.

We present our own framework, based on a general management perspective, in Chapter 3. The purpose of most benefit frameworks, including Figure 1.3, is to provide insights into current IT benefits. Ours has been designed to do more by giving a comprehensive listing of business benefits.

The changing role of evaluation

The previous sections have explained why evaluating the costs and benefits of IT projects is currently a major issue for senior general managers. Many organizations report that they are uncertain how to measure the impact of their IT investments.

The problem is that IT evaluation is caught in a pincer movement. As the amount spent on IT increased, value for money would in any case have been a concern, but the real issue is that the role of IT has changed from one of support to one of strategic importance.

When the purpose of an investment is to support an efficiency drive, the benefits of reduced cost and headcount may be quantifiable in cash flow terms. A technique such as 'return on investment' (ROI) is the natural choice since it is in widespread use for evaluating other types of capital expenditure. However, ROI is unable to capture many of the qualitative benefits that IT brings.

Organizations are now faced with evaluating the range of benefits described above. How can they compare a strategic investment in an IT infrastructure which has a range of intangible and uncertain benefits with other corporate investments whose benefits are more tangible? What measure can be given to the value of locking in suppliers or customers? Where does the actual business benefit of better management information lie? It is small wonder that a tension between advocates of IT-induced change and those who have to approve the investment in the change sometimes surfaces.

The apparent success of ROI for non-IT projects has led organizations to search for some other single technique which can deal with all IT projects in all circumstances. This quest for the 'one best method' is proving fruitless because the range of circumstances to which that technique would have to be applied is so wide that no one technique can cope, even though some authors have claimed that the method they espouse provides the answer for all situations. A primary objective of this book is to show that the characteristics of a project and its organizational environment affect the way an investment decision is handled and therefore indicate which of several available techniques might be suitable for a particular investment.

The problem is really one of alignment. Those organizations that are aware of IT's new role have usually made efforts to incorporate IT in their strategic thinking (see Figure 1.4). This is of little value, however,

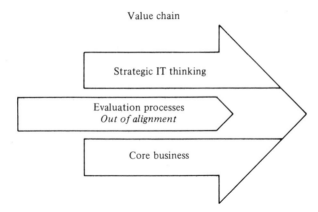

Figure 1.4 Evaluation alignment

if the corporate processes which implement strategy and make it succeed are not aligned with the strategic thinking. An organization that simultaneously boasts of applying strategic IT and of considering only hard quantifiable benefits applied to ROI analysis as the basis for appraising its IT investments is out of alignment. The processes which should make strategic IT work are probably preventing it happening.

Conclusion

This book's thesis is that IT's role is changing from one of automating support functions in a quest for greater efficiency to one where core business processes are being transformed and wider strategic benefits sought, thus giving new impetus to an old problem. This does not mean that the traditional application of IT to support functions has ceased. It has not. A recent report[8] suggested that two thirds of IT investments are still directed at non-core activities. At the same time many organizations are asking their IT managers why this is so when, they believe, greater benefits can be found elsewhere. However, the implication for evaluation is that the techniques used must be able to handle a range of different project types.

The value in studying how to evaluate IT investments is not just being able to say yes or no with greater discrimination. It is that evaluation provides a driving force for the implementation of successful strategic IT. Evaluation gives an understanding of what IT can and cannot do. Better evaluation processes would surely have made a difference to some of the IT disasters that have been reported. At the same time, how many excellent, competitive-advantage-achieving IT investments have been blocked by poor evaluation?

Notes and references

1 In 1961 the IFIP (International Federation for Information Processing) conference on the value of data processing discussed the topic under the heading of Auditing. The proceedings were published as Frielink, A. B. (ed.) (1961) *Auditing Automatic Data Processing*, Elsevier, Amsterdam.

2 Morris, W. E. M. (1971) *Economic Evaluation of Computer Based Systems (Book 1 Working Party Report; Book 2 Workshop Report)*, NCC, Manchester.

3 Frielink, A. B. (ed.) (1975) *Economics of Informatics*, North Holland, Amsterdam.

4 Emery, J. C. (ed.) (1976) *We Can Implement Cost Effective Systems Now*, EDUCOM, Princeton, New Jersey.

5 Bjorn-Andersen, N. and Davis, G. (1988) *IS Assessment: Issues and Challenges*, North Holland, Amsterdam.

6 Scott Morton, M. (ed.) (1991) *The Corporation of the 1990s: Information Technology and Organizational Transformation*, Oxford University Press, New York and Oxford.

7 Stopford, J., Strange, S. with Henley, J. S. (1992) *Rival States, Rival Firms*, Cambridge University Press, Cambridge.

8 Nairn, G. (1988) Going for IT. *Informatics*, July, 34–44.

2 Information technology – why evaluate?

Why is evaluation important?

It is not only IT evaluation that is in doubt, but the value of the systems supported by the technology. Sceptics, such as Lester Thurow, Dean of the Sloan School, continue to throw doubt on the reality of the economic achievement of investments in IT:

1 Investment in IT is high. For many enterprises expenditure on IT has been rising and IT is now one of the most consistent and highest spenders of capital.

   If senior management is to accept and commit itself to the continuous increase in the use of IT it must be convinced that an economic case can be made for the investment.

2 IT is only one of many alternative claims on the enterprise's resources. Management has to be able to compare the returns of investments into a great variety of different ventures in order to achieve the right mix of investments.

   It is equally important to determine the priorities between a range of alternative IT projects.

3 Evaluation provides the benchmarks for what is to be achieved in economic, operational or organizational terms from the investment in IT. Subsequently the benchmarks can be used to provide a measure of the success of the actual implementation of the IT projects.

4 Some form of evaluation is always taking place. If no formal evaluation process exists to inform managers, they will make judgements guided only by their own perceptions. It is better to base decisions on a well-constructed formal evaluation process than to rely on purely subjective judgements. Without such a process there is no common basis for managers to achieve agreement on what actions are appropriate for the enterprise.

In a sense all evaluation is instrumental. It is used by the organization as a way to unite around a set of explicit common goals. Evaluation establishes the measures and, it is hoped, the motivation to achieve

1. ECONOMICS   BEGG - FISCHER - DORNBUSCH
   2nd ED   McGRAW HILL

2. POSITIVE ECONOMICS   LIPSEY
   7th ED   WEIDENFELD PAPERBACKS.

3. ECONOMICS STATISTICS & ECONOMETRICS   T.W. MIRER
   2nd ED   MAXWELL MACMILLAN

4. MATHEMATICS FOR MODERN ECONOMICS   BIRCHENHALL & GROUT.
   PHILIP ALLAN.
   RICHARD BORNAT

19. LINEAR ALGEBRA   S. LIPSCHUTZ   SCHAUM McGRAW HILL.

20. COMPLEX VARIABLES 2ND ED   M.R. SPIEGEL   SCHAUM McGRAW HILL.

21. FUNDAMENTALS OF MATHEMATICS ANALYSIS   R. HAGGARTY   ADDISON WESLEY.

22. MATHEMATICAL ANALYSIS   D. STIRLING   ELLIS HORWOOD.

23. CALCULUS & DIFF. & INTEGRAL VARIAB...

these. Those evaluation techniques which focus on the process of establishing goals and values seek to do so in order to achieve a consensus on the direction the organization is to take.

Why is evaluation regarded as a problem?

The cost side

1 A significant proportion of IT costs are fixed and independent of utilization. Allocating costs to a specific information systems project may be arbitrary. For example, who should bear the costs of constructing a corporate data base, or installing a corporate data and communications network?

2 Even with modern cost estimation tools, estimating the costs of developing major applications is still difficult and unreliable. Cost overruns of several multiples of the original estimate are still too common.

3 Lifetime costs are difficult to estimate because the life of a new system is uncertain – technological obsolescence and changing requirements make it increasingly hazardous to provide a reliable estimate of the system's life.

4 The project champion tends to have a strong attachment to and belief in the ultimate worth of the project under review. Hence champions frequently underestimate costs in order to increase the chance of the project being accepted. Underestimates may be deliberate attempts at deception or merely optimistic accounts of potential costs.

Equally a counter-champion has reason to exaggerate the likely costs of the system to try to prevent its acceptance by the decision makers.

The benefits side

1 Many applications are targeted at achieving second-order effects. Providing better information for a decision maker may improve her decision-making capability. But it is difficult to predict the extent to which the improved information will actually lead to better decisions, and even if it does have the desired effect, putting any kind of value on the better decision may present a new range of problems.

Because it is so difficult to prove that better decisions will be taken, or in retrospect have been taken, sceptics have been able to deny the impact of IT on managerial productivity. There is some evidence that the critical success factor in translating better information into higher managerial productivity is managerial competence – a good manager will utilize the better information to add value to the enterprise. A less good manager will miss out on the possibilities. Indeed, IT can make bad matters worse.

Similar problems can arise where the application is intended to improve the quality of customer service. What value is added by reducing the time taken to process an insurance claim by three days? The impact on cash flow may be negative, whilst it is difficult to estimate the impact on market share. But even an improvement in market share may not result in an improvement in shareholder value or even in the bottom line, if the extra business gained is not profitable.

2 In many cases, the change which is to be evaluated is a major reorganization in which IT may play a role, *but it is the investment in the reorganization as a whole which has to be evaluated.* Such reorganizations take place all the time in a progressive enterprise. It may be a reorganization of the distribution system, or the introduction of a new manufacturing strategy based on just-in-time (JIT), or the absorption of a freshly taken-over competitor which has to be evaluated. It may not be possible to establish JIT working without a significant investment in IT systems, but what proportion of the value added by going JIT should be solely ascribed to the new IT system?

3 The benefits from investments in IT infrastructure are difficult to evaluate. Whilst some of the use which the infrastructure will support can be anticipated and hence evaluated, much of it will develop through time in a somewhat unpredictable way. The introduction of a computer network may have unpredictable effects on the way that office work is organized.

4 Even where the investment targets cost savings – e.g. a reduction in headcount – the actual savings realized from reducing the work content of the office staff by, say, 15%, are unlikely to reduce the headcount by 15%. Fractional savings cannot be aggregated to provide realistic real savings.

5 The common view that an IT system that copes with 80–90% of the requirements for a particular system will yield satisfactory returns on investment may well turn out to be misleading. Once implemented it becomes apparent that the 10–20% remaining outside the IT system incurs 80–90% of the expenditure, or that the cost of keeping the two systems synchronized more than eats up the benefit from the IT system.

6 Two problems which increase the difficulty of estimating benefits stemming from information systems investments are:[1]
   (a) the inherent uncertainty as to outcomes. This point is taken further in Chapter 3.

(b) the difficulty of differentiating the outcomes of alternative designs. 'People approach problems with different experiences, cognitive elements, goals, values and priorities.'[1] As a result outcomes are difficult to define and the probabilities of any one of a number of outcomes materializing are about equal (equivocality).

7 Those who champion the investment proposal have an in-built commitment to the investment. They have already, intuitively or by means of analysis, satisfied themselves of its worth. Research into the role played by champions in the successful implementation of information systems has shown that one of the most important characteristics of champions is their determination to overcome all obstacles. 'Information technology champions are managers who actively and vigorously promote their personal vision for using information technology, pushing the project over or around approval and implementation hurdles.'[2]

Hence they will use any method, including overly optimistic estimates of benefits, to persuade the organization's decision makers to accept the investment proposal.

The counter-champion, on the other hand, who, for whatever reason, opposes the proposal will attempt to denigrate the likely benefits and draw attention to risks and implementation problems.

When do we need to evaluate?

A much-used model of information systems development and operation depicts the progress of information systems through time in the form of an endlessly repeating life-cycle. A system is conceived (perhaps through a managerial visioning process, perhaps because the business has no option but to introduce a new system), undergoes a number of stages of development and assessment, is brought into operation, and when no longer economic to use is replaced by a newer system.

Although earlier versions of the life-cycle model are nowadays being questioned and replaced by models which see the progress of a system through time in a less deterministic fashion, each system is still seen as progressing from conception to operation by means of a number of stages in each of which defined activities take place. In the newer models the order of the stages is no longer as firm. Stages can overlap or proceed in parallel. The whole process contains many iterations, as processes carried out earlier have to be repeated in order to accommodate unanticipated changes or make good failures stemming from earlier errors or misconceptions. The newer models, too, permit experimentation in a number of the development stages.

We can look at the life-cycle model from two viewpoints. The first is from the viewpoint of the *reactive* organization. Changes to existing systems are only contemplated as a response to problems. The problems may stem from pressures outside the business itself – e.g. the arrival of a new competitor, the need to comply with a new law or regulation – or from pressures inside the business – e.g. the existing system can no longer cope with the increasing volume of business. The second viewpoint is that of the *proactive* organization. The organization is always searching for ways of improving its effectiveness and standing in the marketplace, perhaps by organizational change, by the introduction of new products, or by improving the quality of its services. Proactive organizations tend to be the leaders in innovation in their sector, though it does not follow that they also have the highest profitability or show the highest returns to their shareholders.

In the banking sector two organizations which can be classed as proactive, and demonstrated technological leadership, but produced very different results for their shareholders, are City Corporation (Citibank) and Bank of America.

The life-cycle of evaluation

The first phase of the life-cycle model is different in each case.

1 For the *reactive* organization the life-cycle starts with a problem. Problem identification is the first evaluative process needed. Management has to provide some measure of the problem situation – of how the organization might be affected by the problem, of the scale of the problem, of the urgency with which the problem has to be resolved, and of what will happen if the problem is not tackled now. If the problem is to be dealt with in an effective way some kind of consensus on the validity of the evaluation must be achieved in the organization. Without such a consensus it may prove impossible to rectify the problem situation. In practice, as Peter Checkland[3] has shown, in many problem situations problem identification itself proves elusive and is often difficult.

The *proactive* organization is constantly searching for strategies which can improve its standing.[4] It regards IT as one of the weapons it can deploy to achieve its strategic goals. It is constantly reviewing its position and evaluating or re-evaluating new options. The proactive organization tends to look to the future and be very aware of forecasting and planning horizons. As a result it evaluates scenarios of the future and sets out strategic plans in the context of the preferred scenarios which provide a focus and motivation for the organization's activities.

2 Once the presenting problem (for the reactive organization) and the strategic plan (for the proactive organization) are understood and there is some kind of consensus on their nature and measure, management has to define a solution for the problems or an agenda for the strategic plans which will take the organization from evaluated goals and targets into the stages of establishing in greater detail what the new capabilities or facilities are to provide and when the changes need to be made.

The evaluation now concentrates on providing information which enables management to:

(a) satisfy itself that the chosen solution or strategy is feasible – for example, that the organization has the resources and skills
(b) identify the obstacles which might make the chosen course of action difficult or even impossible to achieve
(c) choose between alternative solutions or designs
(d) assess the risk of, on the one hand, not going ahead with any of the proposals (maintaining the *status quo*), and on the other hand, going ahead with the proposals despite elements of uncertainty as to outcomes
(e) establish benchmarks of the likely costs (development and operation) and benefits of the new system
(f) satisfy itself that the case for going ahead is sound, by the criteria acceptable to the management of the organization.

It is the last of these which has engaged practitioners and academics in most discussion. What kind of evaluation is needed to satisfy management that the case is sound? Many evaluation techniques and processes of evaluation have been suggested to enable organizations to make the correct choices. Some of these are discussed in Chapters 7 and 8.

3 In the earlier stages evaluation is concerned with setting targets and predicting outcomes – outcomes in terms of benefits, costs, risks and obstacles. Once a proposal has gained acceptance it becomes a project and the attention of management turns to control. However, evaluation is still very much concerned with prediction. As the project goes through stages of detailed design, technical implementation, testing and transfer into the workplace, predictions of development costs become more precise and more reliable. If experimental techniques such as prototyping are used, estimates of benefits and operating costs, too, become more precise and reliable.

During the systems development phase, one of the principal functions of evaluation is to aid the project manager to manage and control the project. Project costs and schedules should be under constant review with comparisons of estimates and outcomes, and the impact of changes, to enable the project manager to adjust resources and schedules in order to meet the project budget. Evaluation will range from performance evaluation of individuals and groups active in the project, including the performance of subcontractors, to evaluating the precise impact of a late change of requirements called for by client managers on resources and schedules.

4 Once the new system has been tested and assessed by its developers as ready for operational use, the system's users may wish to assure themselves that the system performs according to specification. They will evaluate the systems performance in terms of functionality – does it perform the functions set out in the specification – and in terms of performance – can the system handle the specified volumes and traffic and carry out its function at the expected rates of throughput and response time? Only when the system performs to their satisfaction may they be willing to accept responsibility for the system. It is important that during the period of development, the users constantly review and adjust the benchmarks of expected outcome measures established earlier, in order to ensure that they remain realistic as more information about performance and functionality becomes available.

5 The textbooks suggest that once a system has been implemented in the workplace and comes into operational use an *ex post* evaluation should be carried out. Since carrying out such an evaluation can be costly in terms of both resources used and disruption and disturbance in the workplace – whether the workplace be the directors' boardroom or the shop floor – there needs to be a strong case for engaging in the activity.

The most frequently found reasons for carrying out *ex post* evaluations are:

(a) to ensure that the benefits planned for at the level of the individual, the work group, and the organizational unit are in fact being delivered.

The mere fact that it is known that a post-implementation audit is to be carried out is regarded as a good way of focusing stakeholders' attention on the system and its expected benefits. The audit can act as a spur to ensuring that the intentions behind the new system are being realized. Of course, the impact might be somewhat different in that the users might deliberately 'manufacture' evidence that the system is delivering its benefits.

In a similar manner the costs of operating and maintaining the system should be audited. Run-away costs can destroy the economic case even for a system that seems to be meeting its benchmarked target benefits. The value of the audit lies in reinforcing the message that costs must be tightly controlled. The audit can reveal slack practices.

(b) to identify unforeseen or unexpected benefits or costs. Experience suggests that all innovations have unexpected consequences. Some benefit the organization, and some are dysfunctional. It is important to identify these.

The unexpected benefits can be built on in order to make the most of them – perhaps by exporting the system to other parts of the organization. Those organizations which have benefited strategically from new information systems are often the ones which have been able to recognize and exploit the unexpected outcomes from the new system.

Dysfunctional outcomes have to be carefully examined to see what needs to be done to avoid damage to the organization. Dysfunctional impacts have in the past played an important part in destroying enterprises.

Perhaps the most spectacular unforeseen consequence in recent years was the impact on the London Stock Exchange of the introduction of electronic trading in October 1986. Trading on the floor of the Stock Exchange became rapidly, but unexpectedly, obsolete and had to be abandoned for the trading of shares.

(c) Post-implementation evaluation provides a valuable learning experience about the effectiveness of the cost assessment methods used to estimate project development costs and about the way people in the organization respond to technology-based systems. This knowledge should help with estimating the impacts of future systems.

Post-implementation audits are normally carried out in one or more of three ways:

(a) By establishing the degree of user satisfaction with the new systems.[5] Systems are expected to deliver benefits to their users. It is assumed that if users express satisfaction then the system must be delivering the hoped-for benefits. However, whilst it is true that a system that does not satisfy users cannot be achieving desired goals, the opposite is not necessarily true, and in any case it is not easy to substantiate the claim that user satisfaction is transformed into organizational performance.

(b) By measuring the usage of the system.[6] Where the use of the system is mandatory, percentage use of the system is not relevant. Measurement should focus on the quality of use with measures such as user-caused error rates, and promptness and reliability in using the system. Where the use is discretionary a high usage suggests that users prefer to use the new system and are satisfied that it delivers benefits to them. Low usage suggests that the system fails to deliver the hoped-for benefits and is failing.

(c) By measuring actual performance in terms of the performance benchmarks established at the specification stage of the project.[7] Performance indicators may be expressed in financial terms – the system is expected to save a specific dollar amount or generate an extra DM sales revenue, or increase profitability by a given percentage – or it may be expressed in operational terms – the factory is expected to achieve a growth in output per shift of a certain quantity. Barbara Farbey has suggested that users should engage in a process of self-assessment to establish the impact of new systems or facilities such as workstations on their performance.[8] Without benchmarks such performance evaluation is difficult. On the other hand the use of benchmarks can inhibit the discovery of the often crucial unexpected benefits.

The advantage of the first two measures is that there is a direct relationship between user satisfaction and the quality and quantity of use with the system under review. The output measures of performance, however, are indirect measures subject to a wide range of other influences. An increase in sales may be due to many factors, other than the introduction of the new system.

The total quality measurement (TQM) movement has provided a number of ways of defining and measuring quality. Some of the techniques developed under the umbrella of TQM provide useful ways of maintaining a constant evaluation of the quality of both the development process and the information system as a product.[9]

6 Throughout its life a system is subject to alterations. These arise because faults are discovered in a system and need to be corrected, because the performance of the system is inadequate in terms such as response time or number of users able to use the system at one time, or because the functions performed by the system have to be altered in the context of changing requirements. Each change has to be evaluated and treated in a similar way to the evaluation carried out when the system was first conceived. Again changes can be reactive or proactive.

7 At some point the changes become overwhelming and the system is perceived as being at the end of its useful life. Evaluation is concerned with comparing the cost of keeping the old system going with that of constructing a new system. In some cases it has proved impossible to use the old system as a platform for constructing the new or for comparing the two.

8 A very different kind of evaluation has to be carried out from time to time. This is an evaluation of the performance of the IT group as an organizational unit. Does the unit perform up to expectations; does it add value to the organization; should alternative structures for delivering information systems be investigated; should the enterprise

examine the possibilities of subcontracting or outsourcing its IT activities?

9 Information systems and IT incur significant costs which in many organizations are regarded as costs which should be distributed to the users in proportion to either the use they make of the facilities, or the benefits the technology delivers to the users. The problem of charge-out brings out a number of problems related to evaluation. These include problems of allocating joint costs and of sharing benefits which themselves are the product of joint products such as a corporate data base.

This book does not attempt to consider the questions of charging and auditing the IT group in detail, but merely draws attention to the fact that both of these are further facets of the evaluation problem.

Summary

In the previous paragraphs we have indicated some of the problems and challenges inherent in evaluating information systems projects. In the next chapter we go on to put the problems of evaluation in the context of some of the challenges facing the corporation, private or public, in the last decade of the twentieth century.

Notes and references

1 An interesting discussion of these issues is provided in: Cooper, R. B. and Quinn, R. E. (1991) *Management Information System Effectiveness: A Competing Values Perspective*, College of Business Administration Working Paper, University of Houston.

2 A number of researchers have studied the important role of champions in information systems development. An interesting study is that of: Beath, C. (1991) Supporting the information technology champion, *MIS Quarterly,* **15**, No. 3, 355–372.

3 Peter Checkland and his group at Lancaster University have developed an approach to problem identification based on the notion that many organizational problems are viewed very differently by a range of stakeholders, and that many problems do not present themselves in a readily measurable form but the nature of the problem emerges through time. Checkland's position and his 'soft systems methodology' are set out in: Checkland, P. (1981) *Systems Thinking, Systems Practice*, John Wiley and Son. A more recent book, Checkland, P. B. and Scholes, J. (1990) *Soft Systems Methodology in Action*, John Wiley and Son, provides an updated version of the approach based on many situations in which the approach was used.

4 One of the best discussions of how organizations set about proactive strategic planning is provided by: Earl, M. (1987) Information systems strategy formation, in *Critical Issues in Information Systems Research* (eds R. J. Boland and R. A. Hirschheim), Wiley Series in Information Systems, Chichester, pp. 157–178. Further reading is provided by: Scott Morton, M. (ed.) (1991) *The Corporation of the 1990s: Information Technology and Organizational Transformation*, Oxford University Press. The book provides an

account of some of the more important findings of the major research project carried out by MIT with the collaboration of 12 major corporations.

5 There have been a number of studies using the user satisfaction measure. Some have used measures of satisfaction of the system's performance – timeliness and accuracy – and others have focused on satisfaction with softer aspects such as the system's user friendliness. A good review of effectiveness criteria is provided in: Hamilton, S. and Chervany, N. L. (1981) Evaluating information systems effectiveness – Part I: Comparing evaluation approaches, *MIS Quarterly,* **5**, No. 3, 55–69.

6 A number of researchers have used the usage model for post-implementation evaluation. These include: Scrinivasan, A. (1985) Alternative measures of system effectiveness: associations and implications, *MIS Quarterly,* **9**, No. 3, pp. 243–253.

7 Most performance measures have focused on economic returns. A centre for research on methods of evaluating the impact of information systems on economic performance has been Carnegie-Mellon University. See, for example, Kriebel, C. H. and Raviv, A. (1980) An economics approach to modelling the productivity of computer systems, *Management Science,* **26**, No. 3, 29–34.

8 Barbara Farbey has studied the impact of workstation use amongst professional and information system users in an international high-technology company. The company had provided its workers with a very high per capita value of IT facilities. It had assumed that the use of the facilities would enhance the productivity of its already high-productivity workers. However, the company had little idea what the real impact on performance was, or how to explain the business benefits, let alone measure them.

9 Frank Land and Richard Tweedie have suggested that TQM methods and methods derived from information systems development methodologies could be combined to provide a valuable toolkit for the evaluation of quality in IT systems development. See: Land, F. and Tweedie, R. (1992) *Preparing for Information Technology Implementation: Adding a TQM Structure,* Bond University Working Paper, Gold Coast, Queensland

3 The great information systems benefit hunt

Introduction

The introduction of major new information systems is a difficult and uncertain business. It is uncertain because an information system affects the organization in a variety of ways and along a number of dimensions, many of which are poorly understood.

One crucial dimension, which gives rise to much uncertainty, is that of the costs, benefits and disbenefits of introducing a new system.

The uncertainty has many sources:

- Organizations are often simply *unaware* of the costs, benefits and disbenefits which result from instituting a major new system.
- Many projects represent *new ways of doing things* – they are, in the context into which they are introduced, innovatory, and, for that reason, novel.
- *The planning horizon* – the period for current plans to be implemented, is *longer than the forecasting horizon*. It is impossible to forecast with any accuracy what the world will be like at the time the system is to be implemented.
- Even when the organization is aware of the possible costs, benefits and disbenefits, they are often *intangible and difficult to measure*.[1]
- If the most important costs, benefits and disbenefits are difficult to measure (and with a major new system this is the most likely case), it is *difficult to evaluate and to manage* the changes which result.[2]
- The *processes* which are used to evaluate a system may not reveal the softer benefits and the impact which the system may have in human and organizational terms. They may positively obscure them.[3]
- A major new system can, and usually does, unpredictably alter the *social structures and culture of an organization*. It changes some of the ground rules.[4]
- The system may *alter the boundary between an organization and its environment*. Relationships with customers, competitors and suppliers may change.[5,6]

Moreover, as we have seen in Chapter 2:

- Uncertainty in the environment means that it is not possible to foresee how the new system will play itself out. After the initial impact there are second- and higher order effects which interact with each other to give rise to quite unpredictable results. These are what are called *emergent effects*.
- New systems are often introduced as part of a greater change programme. It may be impossible to determine which of the changes led to a particular outcome, and indeed an effect may be only attributable to the joint action of all the changes. This *uncertainty of attribution* may also follow if the information systems change coincides with other, non-related changes.
- Where a new system serves a number of groups (perhaps different profit centres) it is difficult to allocate costs, and hence net benefits, to each user.

As a result, the benefits which were expected and provided the motivation for introducing the systems may not be realized. Benefits which might have been there for the taking go unrecognized, and are missed. News of the benefits may not filter upwards, or across. Some benefits are lost through mismanagement. Some are lost because the conditions which made them attractive no longer exist.

Sometimes the benefit cannot be reaped without further changes. For example, the full benefits from implementing electronic data interchange (EDI) may not emerge until the way that the work of progress chasers is organized is rearranged.

Other benefits which do accrue are totally unexpected. A lack of awareness of different types and levels of benefit can lead to an incomplete realization of the full, potential benefit of a system, as when the operational levels of an organization milk the benefits of efficiency, but senior management miss the possible strategic benefits.

Costs and benefits are the focus of any evaluation but before they can be evaluated, costs and benefits must first be recognized for what they are. Our research has shown that the scope of benefits varied widely from project to project and that a simple, comprehensive list of the benefits which had been achieved, or failed to be achieved, would in itself be welcomed. This was true even in companies which could be considered as sophisticated IT users. This chapter contains lists of both costs and benefits, compiled, in the main, from the research study and supplemented by other lists of costs and benefits reported in the literature.

It has been possible, however, to go one stage further and make a first attempt at devising a framework for classifying the benefits. The framework, presented next, is derived from consolidating and adapting a number of existing frames, principally that of the structure of an organization from Mintzberg's *Structure in Fives*.[7]

The chapter finishes with a preliminary discussion of why organizations are not achieving possible benefits, illustrated with reference to the research study. The discussion is taken forward in Chapter 5, which presents some longer case studies and identifies some prerequisites for successful information system implementation and evaluation.

A framework for classifying benefits

There are two reasons why having a framework on which to classify benefits is helpful. First, having a framework helps to organize the list of benefits. Second, having a framework acts as a prompt. It is possible to tease out potential new areas by noticing which parts of the framework appear to have been already addressed in the introduction of new systems, and which have not. The latter may suggest new possibilities.

The framework used to classify benefits is constructed by analogy with the model of organizational structure described in Mintzberg's *Structure in Fives*.[7]

Mintzberg's description of an organization

Mintzberg describes the basic parts of an organization as shown in Figure 3.1.

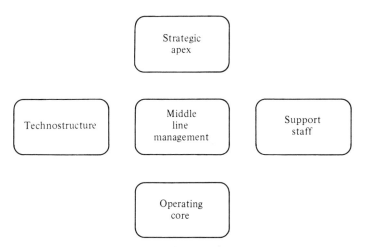

Figure 3.1 The basic parts of an organization. (Adapted from Mintzberg, 1983)

In constructing the original framework, Mintzberg's main concern was to differentiate the 'component parts of an organisation and the *people* contained in each'. His description of the important features of each part are summarized in Table 3.1.

Table 3.1 The five basic parts of an organization – a summary

Strategic apex: includes people charged with overall responsibility for the organization
Middle line: includes the chain of middle managers running from senior management to first-line supervisors
Operating core: includes people who perform the basic work related directly to the production of products and services
Technostructure: includes people who serve the organization by affecting the work of other people
Support staff: includes people who provide support for the organization outside the basic flow of work. These are often specialists

In constructing the framework, we have focused on differentiating the *purposes* of each component part. Arguing by analogy, the different purposes for which new information systems are introduced have been imposed on Mintzberg's 'people' structure. Following Mintzberg the purposes are named: strategic, management, operational, technostructure/functionality and support. They are taken in turn.

Strategic

Mintzberg suggests that the strategic apex has three sets of duties: direct supervision, management of the organization's boundary conditions and the development of the organization's strategy. It is the part of the organization that 'takes the widest, and as a result the most abstract, perspective of the organisation'. Following this lead, those benefits which are abstract, wide-ranging, and which affect the organization as a whole are classified as 'strategic'.

Management

The duties of middle-line managers include the collection, aggregation and passing of information, as well as decision-making and the allocation of resources. Like managers in the strategic apex, these managers are concerned with boundary management, but at the level of the unit. Again following Mintzberg's lead and considering the purpose for which the systems were intended or used, those benefits which support these particular duties are classified as 'management'. Further, from the empirical research it appeared that managers were much concerned with the management and development of their staff. These concerns have been added to the 'management' category.

Operational: efficiency and effectiveness

Benefits were classified as 'operational' where the computer technology was introduced to support the basic work of the organization. The distinction between 'operational' and 'support' (below) can be illustrated by the case of one of the organizations in the study which was a technical publishing company. Their products were technical documents produced by teams of authors. Benefits which the company related to more efficient working of their technical authors were classified as 'operational' because they sprang from improvements to one of the core processes of production; the production of technical documents. Benefits which arose because the authors could communicate more easily with the company, e.g. through being on-line, were classified as 'support'.

Technostructure/functionality

Mintzberg's definition of the technostructure includes people whose function it is to influence the *way* in which people work, e.g. operations researchers or work-study teams. The research showed that new computer-based systems enabled new ways of working, or allowed people to do things which were not feasible under the old regime. In other words the systems affected work process and work content to give greater functionality. The benefits which arose from this were classified as 'technostructure/functionality'.

Support

The analogy holds up well for four out of five of the Mintzberg categories. Strategic, middle management, operational and technostructure benefits are all identifiable without stretching the analogy too far.

It begins to be rather strained, however, when considering the purposes which are associated with support staff. Such staff are '. . . units, all specialised, that exist to provide support to the organisation outside its operating work flow.'

Clinging to the analogy for the moment, one is looking for information systems, possibly specialized, whose purpose it is to provide 'support to the organisation outside its operating work flow'. An example is electronic mail. A facility for sending and receiving mail electronically is exactly analogous to the work of the mailroom, classified by Mintzberg as support. There is something to be said for the argument that all provision of infrastructure is inherently a support function. As another example, some external data bases, such as credit-rating data bases, are generally used outside the normal flow of work.

However, the distinction between 'operational' and 'support' is not always clear. Is using a credit-rating data base definitely a support, or is it a way to make the flow of customer information processing more efficient for the processing clerk? Is word-processing a support application for managers, providing secretarial support? Or does it provide an operational benefit, enabling him or her to do the job of managing more efficiently? It could be that one person's support is another's operational efficiency and that the answer is conditional, only to be found with respect to a real situation.

A summary of the classification is included in Table 3.2.[8] Clearly this is a useful rather than a watertight classification. The classes overlap and most new systems have impacts across several categories. Other models of organization and purpose will give different classes. Perhaps the important point is that any attempt to make sense of the impact of a new system, and its associated jumble of benefits, disbenefits and costs, will have some underlying model. It is better to have that model explicit.

Table 3.2 A classification system for IT benefit: category definitions

Strategic benefits include those associated with:

Development of the organization's strategy
Management of the organization's boundaries
Internal integration
Business process redesign
Business network redesign
Business scope definition
Competitive advantage
Developing new business

Management benefits include those associated with:

Collection of information on the performance of the manager's unit
Aggregation and passing of information up the hierarchy
Better decision-making
Allocation of resources
Management of the unit's boundary
Management and development of people

Table 3.2 cont.

Operational efficiency and effectiveness benefits include those associated with:

Securing of inputs
Transformation of inputs into outputs
Distribution of outputs
Direct support to input, output and transformation functions
Localized exploitation
Improved productivity and performance
Transforming outputs into desired outcomes

Functionality benefits include those associated with:

Changes to the way in which work is done
Standardization
Changes of functions and tasks
Rationalization of tasks
New ways of managing and organizing

Support benefits include those associated with:

Infrastructure which provides supporting systems outside the operational
    sphere, like electronic mail

Information benefits include those associated with:

Better information for tasks and for taking decisions

Communication benefits include those associated with:

Improved mutual understanding
Extension of the range of ideas which are commonly understood
Changing the symbols and the image of the organization
Clarification of communication breakdowns
More democratic consensus-finding and decision-taking
Improved dialogue

Learning benefits include:

New mental models of the organization
New mental models of the organization's environment, including other related
    organizations such as customers and suppliers
New learning
New learning how to learn
Shared learning

Information, communication and organizational learning

Mintzberg's *Structure in Fives* is one way to consider benefits, taking an
organizational perspective. An alternative view takes an information
systems perspective with an emphasis on 'informing', 'communications'
and 'learning' as shown in the bottom portion of Table 3.2. It is worth

distinguishing between two kinds of 'information' used to support organizational activity. The first is of the sort carried in organizational data bases, or in external data bases. This use of the term 'information' carries with it a sense of being packaged, a scent of libraries and data bases and the (potential) benefits of 'better information'. Such information is used, for example, in decision making.

But there is another kind of support information, namely the information that is *about* the organization and its environment, about what one needs to know to operate *within* an organizational environment and beyond it. Here the sense is of 'meta-information': the formal and informal structures of the organization, its rules, its culture, the meaning of words and phrases used in the organization – the jargon. It includes rules and understandings of how relationships with customers, suppliers and other external stakeholders are regulated. This kind of information evolves through political and social processes and is (largely) carried by informal systems.

IT, more particularly computer-based communications technology, affects such processes and is affected by them but they are essentially human processes and evolve through communication between people. The (potential) benefits are those of better 'communication'. They would include, for example, benefits which come from improved mutual understanding, or from clarification of terms leading to improved dialogue. Another example of benefits to be gained from improved communication would be the ability to involve more people in decision making, using say E-mail, thereby creating a better consensus for subsequent action. Or it might be possible through better and faster communication to create an improved image of the organization internally, with staff, or externally, with customers.

A special form of (potential) benefit is that which enables learning and, going down a further level, learning how to learn. Benefits from this use of information could be called 'cognitive'. They alter the way in which it is possible to perceive and to think about the organization in its environment. Simulation and strategic modelling are examples of this kind of use of the technology.[9]

Information and communication benefits are all potentially to be had from IS and they are to be sought across all the classes. The broad classificatory system is now complete.

A catalogue of benefits

A list of benefits, compiled from the research and from other sources, is presented in Figures 3.2, 3.3 and 3.4 based the 'Mintzberg' classification.

Strategic

- long- or short-term viability of the organization
- existing system has become inadequate
- 'got to do'
- provide systems that would make them unique to customers
- demonstrate knowledge and understanding of high technology and the high-technology marketplace
- support for the company's strategy or mission
- permit new forms of organization

Support

- improved communications
- provision of infrastructure systems
- compatibility with customer's systems
- common report formats
- the system was necessary to enable the organization to meet, or respond quickly to, changes in the law
- changes in corporate strategy can be easily documented
- common pool of management information leading to better decision-making

Management

- increased flexibility
- modernization
- standardization
- better control
- more effective use of the sales force
- growing the skills of the workforce
- meeting the highest professional standards
- ease of operation, allowing inexperienced staff to be employed
- remove pressure for regrading
- greater professional control of work
- improving the quality of working life

Functional

- bringing facilities in-house
- providing internal support systems
- integration of information from a variety of sources
- better account handling
- ability to handle increased product complexity
- eliminating the distance barrier: office to office, office to home, office to customer or supplier

Operational

- more effective use of existing kit
- improved quality at reduced cost
- improved turnaround time
- 'headcount' reduction
- reduction in printing costs
- reduction in storage costs
- reduction in property costs
- increased income from better quality product
- timeliness and accessibility of data
- timeliness (general)
- speed
- better graphics
- accuracy
- adding value to data
- less duplication of information
- growth without corresponding increase in overheads

Figure 3.2 Motivation for the introduction of IT

Figure 3.2, taken from the research case studies, shows those benefits which provided the motivation in practice for embarking on new information systems as they were seen by the organizations.

Strategic benefits

At the highest level in the framework are those motivated by strategic necessity. In at least two of the cases studied, the very existence of the business unit as a separate entity had been at stake. Using the technology, they had reckoned to improve quality and cut costs sufficiently to contend successfully with market threats. In one case, the threat came from small, independent companies with potentially lower costs. In the other, a public sector organization, the threat was from 'contracting out' the work of the unit.

A related impetus came from a perception that existing systems were inadequate for the company's present or future growth. A service company wanting to spread geographically needed an infrastructure to grow and provide economies of scale. In other companies this was expressed as a 'got-to-do', i.e. the company was persuaded that only by using the technology could they maintain the quality of service and presentation available elsewhere in the industry.

Other strategic reasons included the provision of systems that would make them unique to customers. This included giving customers direct access to parts of the system. A finance house, for example, provided customers with access to portions of the company data base and retrieval facilities. A systems supplier used their own systems to demonstrate their knowledge of and understanding of the high-technology marketplace.

Management

A number of management issues arose when talking about the motivation for introducing new systems. Among these were questions of improved control over the work process, e.g. through keeping the whole processing in-house or through standardization. One of the public sector organizations saw an improvement in turnaround time and a lessening of their dependence on outside contractors as important considerations.

Several of the organizations wanted to use the networking capabilities of the systems to provide electronic links between offices. They wanted to link different parts of the country, and to co-ordinate work. This extended to include electronic links between the organization and their business partners.

There was some recognition, too, that the new systems could be used to enrich some jobs and enhance skills. Secretaries were often mentioned in this context. It was thought that their work could be made more interesting, by drawing on their creative skills in layout and design, rather than typing skills which were seen as more mechanical. In one company, the systems were seen from the start as giving engineers more control over their work.

Operational: efficiency and effectiveness

A whole cluster of motivations revolved around the idea of improved efficiency and effectiveness. These included, for example, timeliness, speed, quality and flexibility.

Most of the organizations had anticipated a saving in time resulting from improved methods of production, including document production. The cycle of proof-reading and correction could be shortened, as could the time taken to 'cut and paste'.

Functionality/technostructure

Several of the organizations were seeking to do new things with their systems, in other words to increase 'functionality'.

Two of the manufacturing organizations, for example, wanted a system which would interface electronically with systems in other departments. A finance house wanted to use the networking capability of the proposed system to allow senior executives to pick up their 'desk tops' from any workstation in the company.

Integration of information from different sources was a primary concern of one of the publishing houses. The material required for the production of technical manuals, for example, came in different forms including text and graphics. It also came in different formats, on diskettes, from suppliers who had incompatible systems. The company therefore saw the ability of the technology to scan in pictures and to support a variety of standard formats as a considerable benefit.

Communication

Compatibility with other systems provided a further motivating factor. Such systems could be either other systems internal to the company, or customer's systems, or both. Issues which arose under this heading were networking, infrastructure provision and integration and standardization.

Integration included both the technical ingtegration of systems and the integration of information from a wide variety of sources.

For example, a pharmaceutical subsidiary had to use a system which was compatible with both its parent company in the US and their manufacturing systems located elsewhere in the UK. The central personnel department of a computer vendor wanted to provide standard formats, content and methods of production across a number of local personnel offices.

By contrast, a financial services company had, in choosing the new system, disregarded head-office requirements for the implementation of a compatible system, because they saw no special value in achieving compatibility. A major software company, organized into autonomous business units, attempted to establish compatible systems across the business units, but failed to persuade many of the units that the technology chosen was appropriate for the work of the units.

A variation on the theme of compatibility was that of 'compliance'. In some cases, for instance in the pharmaceutical and defence industries, particular systems were necessary in order to meet specific legal or contractual requirements.

Less stringent pressures to enhance communication were also in evidence. For example, companies saw the systems as helping them to 'meet the highest professional standards', or as part of a requirement to modernize. Improved quality of presentation was an important motivating factor.

Unplanned benefits

Many of the benefits reported in the studies were unplanned and unexpected and many of the unplanned benefits were found in changed opportunities. They are listed in Figure 3.3. Some were individual; for example, both professional and support staff found that their jobs had been enriched. Others were organizational. In one company the introduction of the system was seen to have acted as a catalyst for reorganization of the management structure. Yet others were social. One informant remarked that he had never expected to see such high technology available to ordinary men and women, so soon.

Some of the unexpected benefits were second-order benefits. For example, a company offering professional services had only grasped the full significance of being able to network their offices after the system was installed. They they found that they were able to switch work between offices to the point where they could take advantage of cheaper labour and real estate costs away from London.

Another found that more timely information meant that they could cut their warehousing costs.

One company found that the successful introduction of the new system had reduced the fear of the technology and had eased the introduction of further systems. In this case the introduction of the

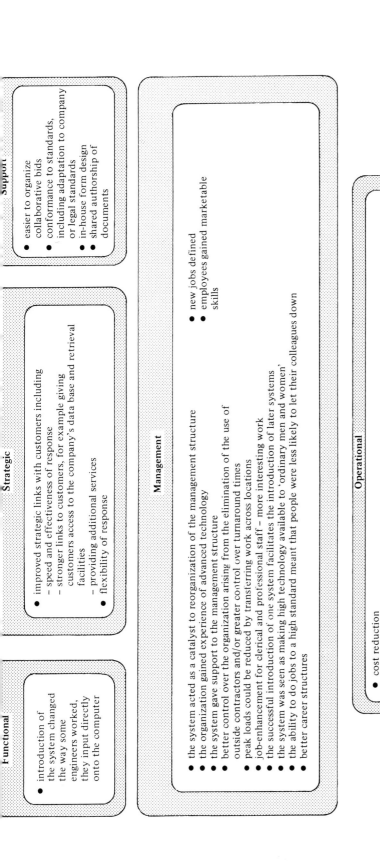

Functional

- introduction of the system changed the way some engineers worked, they input directly onto the computer

Strategic

- improved strategic links with customers including
  - speed and effectiveness of response
  - stronger links to customers, for example giving customers access to the company's data base and retrieval facilities
  - providing additional services
  - flexibility of response

Support

- easier to organize collaborative bids
- conformance to standards, including adaptation to company or legal standards
- in-house form design
- shared authorship of documents

Management

- the system acted as a catalyst to reorganization of the management structure
- the organization gained experience of advanced technology
- the system gave support to the management structure
- better control over the organization arising from the elimination of the use of outside contractors and/or greater control over turnaround times
- peak loads could be reduced by transferring work across locations
- job-enhancement for clerical and professional staff – more interesting work
- the successful introduction of one system facilitates the introduction of later systems
- the system was seen as making high technology available to 'ordinary men and women'
- the ability to do jobs to a high standard meant that people were less likely to let their colleagues down
- better career structures
- new jobs defined
- employees gained marketable skills

Operational

- cost reduction
  - staff costs reduced by transferring work from an expensive location to a cheaper one
  - stationery savings
- greater productivity
- time
  - professional time saved
  - deadlines could be met
- more time could be spent thinking and writing, less on corrections
- improved quality and accuracy of reports and of viewfoils

Figure 3.3 Unplanned benefits

system facilitated the later introduction, using the same technology, of a system designed to support senior executives – a development which previously had been totally rejected.

In contrast to the planned benefits, the unplanned ones showed a rather greater emphasis on intangible, qualitative benefits. This is partly attributable to hindsight, and partly to circumstance. The planned benefits had been defined in the context of justifying expenditure to people, both in the IT function and outside it, who were looking for 'hard' facts to weigh against that expenditure. The unexpected benefits were elicited after the event. Besides, the questions which we asked were likely to bring out intangible as well as tangible benefits.

Figure 3.4 shows a further list of benefits: this time chosen from those that have been discussed in the information systems literature.[10] In comparing the benefits which were reported to us with those which came from the literature, it was noticeable that the latter were more strategic, less tangible. Partly this is because of the way people write journal articles – they have to be, or ought to be, at the frontier. That said, the kinds of benefit currently under discussion in the literature are there as possibilities, as 'stretching' questions, pointing the way to a different level of benefit. More precisely, they point to a different order of magnitude of change, with all the attendant possible benefits and risks.

In practice, this level was often missed.

Why are organizations not achieving possible benefits

Lack of awareness

The research project showed that many of the unexpected benefits were social (i.e. benefits to staff or other people) rather than technical or financial.

In one company, where the system was regarded as a success, it had been installed to improve the efficiency with which reports were brought together and collated. The company had expected to save time in production, in correction, in cutting and pasting diagrams, in collating information from different computers and in easier text and graphics manipulation.

What they had not foreseen was the improvement in creativity gained by authors, who were able to capture 'first thoughts' more easily. Nor had they envisaged the possibilities of shared authorship which the system opened up, or that collaborative bids would be easier to manage.

In another company, a financial services company, planned benefits were very much perceived as internal to the company. They had expected that the quality of information available to executives would

Strategic

- change industry structure and the rules of competition
- create competitive advantage
- enhanced service to create a larger business base
- spawn entirely new businesses
- enhance differentiation
- increase market share
- remove constraints to growth
- new products

- realign the balance in the customer–supplier relationship
- establish barriers to new entrants
- improve the specific content of information products
- improve the selectivity with which information is used
- remove limitations of time and distance
- further globalization

Support

- emancipate organizations from time and distance barriers

Management

- improved security because the whole task is done on site
- reduce the possibility of having to operate in crisis mode
- flatter organization (cutting out layers of management)
- improve management

Operational

- time savings including
  - reduction in time-lags associated with information
  - easier, thus faster, editing
- cost savings, including
  - reduction in operating costs
  - cost of slide and viewfoil production
- good technical manuals can also be revenue earners

Functional

- increase the range of system capabilities, including
  - generality
  - flexibility
  - ability to produce *ad hoc* reports
  - improved services
  - portability (e.g. for presentation graphics)
- quality considerations, including
  - accuracy of output
  - reliability
- usability, including
  - ease of use by non-professionals
  - reduced user costs
  - easier customer acceptance
- new styles of remote working

Figure 3.4 A further tranche of benefits

be better, as would communications within the company. In practice the benefits came from being able to strengthen their links with customers, by providing them with access to the company data bases and information retrieval services. This, they believed, gave them a competitive advantage.

More than half the companies reported that people had found new ways of working, that jobs had been enriched or new posts created. None of these companies had listed these as planned benefits. It seemed to come as something of a surprise, particularly with respect to professional staff.

It is worth noting that lack of awareness of different levels of benefits may be different at different levels of the organization. The operating core may have milked the efficiency benefits but senior management may not have seen the possible strategic benefits.

Management problems

In no case had the implementation of the new systems been without hiccups. Two cases illustrate the kinds of problem that arise. In the first, failure to manage the system once in place had led to significant underutilization (further examples are described in Chapter 5). In the second, the system was being used, but in a very different way to that envisaged.

In the first case the search for an improved system had stemmed from the company's growth plans. The company's offices each had a typing pool which produced reports on typewriters or on stand-alone microcomputers from long-hand originals. The company had no doubt that the existing system was inadequate and would prevent business objectives from being met. Planned benefits from the system were:

- to produce better quality reports
- to allow growth objectives to be met without a large increase in overheads
- to provide links between the offices to permit the transfer of documents *and the co-ordination of activities.*

In the event, the company achieved the first two objectives. However, the full range of facilities provided by having a linked network was not being utilized. Users have kept to the basic facilities they employed at the outset. Also the potential for co-ordination and project planning has not been achieved. In part this is because the person designated as systems administrator, who might have been able to drive these activities, has not been able to give priority to the role and to allocate her time properly. At the time of the interview her secretarial role, including making the tea, was given precedence.

The difference between projected use and actual use

In the second company which had not achieved the expected benefits, the system had been subject to major teething problems. As a result, the system manager had a fairly jaundiced view of the technology. But he was also put out because the usage of the system was very different from that which he had envisaged. Although it was originally intended for the production of bread-and-butter, 'non-glossy' reports, engineers in the company had discovered that the system could be very successfully used for creative work. The greatest benefit was seen by them as the production of quality viewfoils. The manager complained ruefully that some people were 'becoming addicted'.

As was noted in the Introduction, the actual effects of installing a system are uncertain and unpredictable.

Measurement

Difficulty in measuring changes due to the introduction of IT caused problems in evaluating the systems both before and after they were introduced. A particular concern was the way in which organizations approached intangible benefits.

By and large, the inclusion of intangible benefits was not considered acceptable as part of the procedures of evaluation. Very few companies even tried to measure them. At least one of the companies described the investment as 'an act of faith'.

Nevertheless, intangibles had a powerful effect. One company had a very stringent formal procedure for cost justification. Senior management insisted on completion of a formal cost justification document. Where departments or functions could not justify proposals on 'hard-nosed' benefits, applications for investment were refused.

The organization had adapted to the situation in several ways. First, the information systems department was trained to find benefits, through a very careful analysis of objectives, business processes, people costs, information flows and possible synergies with other groups. Second, in at least one instance, when this had failed, the managing director had changed the ground rules and ordered them to look at 'management processes' rather than 'business processes'. The required justification was found. Finally, several of the most senior directors had been able to bypass the system altogether, over a round of golf.

Most of the organizations regarded the efficiency benefits as the major benefits; other 'softer' benefits were seen as a bonus. Perhaps they should have seen them the other way round?

Costs

Like benefits, the costs associated with the introduction of new systems are often intangible. Nevertheless, many of the methods to be discussed in the later chapters of this book call for estimates of cost. Hochstrasser and his colleagues[11] have done valuable research into the costs of information systems. In his work on evaluation he has provided a catalogue of costs incurred in the introduction of a new system. Hochstrasser maintains that the cost of an investment should be broadened to include a range of costs – technological, human, organizational – and should include both primary and secondary effects. He also distinguishes between direct costs and indirect costs. The lists shown in Table 3.3 are taken directly from his work.

Table 3.3 The costs associated with the introduction of new IS

Direct costs

Environmental
Hardware
Installation and configuration
Running costs
Maintenance
Breakdown
Security
Networking
Training
Phasing out

Indirect costs

Management and staff time
Devising, approving and amending plans
Planning, explaining and implementing
Security reviews

Source: Hochstrasser, B. (1990) Evaluating IT investments – matching techniques to projects, *Journal of Information Technology,* **5** (4), 215–221.

Conclusions

The research findings, in the first instance, reinforce the common call for greater IT awareness and education at all levels of the organization. These are necessary both to achieve the full benefits of a new system and to avoid at least the known pitfalls.

Further they have shown that not many people know how well, or how badly, their systems have performed in practice. They do not even have a very clear perception of the issues. As a result, many benefits have gone begging. Benefits have to be managed if they are to be gathered. To manage benefits there must be awareness of where to look for impacts, as well as a process for evaluation and for acting on the results.

There is also the question of the predictive value of different methods of cost justification and evaluation. Methods based only on accounting techniques such as ROI, do not, in themselves, involve a process which will bring out the softer benefits, let alone the impact which the system may have in human and organizational terms. Such methods may actually obscure them.

Methods based on a search process, e.g. those which involve 'multi-objective, multi-criteria' techniques, are much better placed. Such methods are more likely to capture the plurality of interest which attends the introduction of new systems. In so doing they are likely to address a wider range of benefits, and disbenefits, how they interact and how they are distributed. On the one hand the methods act as an education process concerning benefits; on the other they enable management to see what has to be managed.

The issue of defining and measuring the outcomes following the introduction of new information systems is widely regarded as of critical importance. Having a framework helps to organize benefits and costs and can stimulate thoughts on where to look for them. More than that, if the framework is built on an explicit model of how an organization works rather than an implicit one, it becomes possible to challenge the model. It makes it possible to say 'This is Mintzberg's model of an organization. It fits my organization very well in this bit . . . but not in that one. My organization works like this . . .' And it makes it possible to go off on your own Great Benefit Hunt.

Notes and references

1 Rivard, E. and Kaiser, K. (1989) The benefits of quality IS, *Datamation*, 15 January, 53–58.
2 Blackler, R. and Brown, C. (1988) Theory and practice in evaluation, in *IS Assessment: Issues and Challenges* (eds N. Bjorn-Andersen and G. Davis), North Holland, Amsterdam, pp. 351–374.
3 Hirschheim, R. and Smithson, S. (1988) A critical analysis of information system evaluation, in *IS Assessment: Issues and Challenges* (eds N. Bjorn-Andersen and G. Davis), North Holland, Amsterdam, pp. 17–37.
4 Walsham, G. (1990) Structuration theory and information systems research, in *Proceedings of the Eleventh International Conference on Information Systems*,

December 1990, Copenhagen (eds J. DeGross, M. Alavi and H. Oppelland), ACM, Baltimore, pp. 53–59.

5 Rotemberg, J. J. and Saloner, G. (1991) Interfirm competition and collaboration, in *The Corporation of the 1990s: Information Technology and Organisational Transformation* (ed. M. Scott Morton), Chapter 4, Oxford University Press, New York and Oxford.

6 Macdonald, K. H. (1991) Business strategy development, alignment and redesign, in *The Corporation of the 1990s: Information Technology and Organisational Transformation* (ed. M. Scott Morton), Chapter 6, Oxford University Press, New York and Oxford.

7 Mintzberg, H. (1983) *Structure in Fives: Designing Effective Organisations*, Chapter 1, Prentice Hall International Inc, Englewood Cliffs, New Jersey.

8 The original Mintzberg definitions have been stretched to include finer distinctions which come from writings in information systems. Sources which we have used are: Earl, M. (1989) *Management Strategies for Information Technology*, Chapter 1, Prentice Hall, New York and London; Earl, M. and Hopwood, A. (1987) From management information to information management, in *Towards Strategic Information Systems*, Vol. 1 (eds E. Somogyi and R. D. Galliers), Strategic Information Systems Management Series, Abacus Press, Tunbridge Wells and Cambridge, Mass., pp. 93–112; Scott Morton, M. S. (ed.) *The Corporation of the 1990s: Information Technology and Organisational Transformation*, Oxford University Press, New York and Oxford.

9 The May 1992 issue of *The European Journal of Operational Research* (s, 1) is devoted to exploring techniques and methods of 'Modelling for Learning'.

10 Many articles and books refer to IT benefits. Of particular interest are: Ciborra, C. U. (1987) Reframing the role of computers in organisations: the transaction costs approach, *Office: Technology and People*, **3**, 17–38; Emery, J. C. (1971) *Cost Benefit Analysis of Information Systems*, SMIS Workshop Report No. 1, The Society for Information Systems; Hammer, C. (1988) Is today's office receiving full value from its computers? *Information and Management*, **15**, 15–23; Porter, M. E. (1988) *Business Success in the 1990s: What are the Key Issues?* Amdahl Executive Institute, Hartley-Witney, Hampshire; Strassman, P. (1988) Measuring the productivity of technical documentation, *Journal of Information Technology*, **3**, 1; Ward, J. (1986) An appraisal of the competitive benefits of information technology, *Journal of Information Technology*, **1**, 3; Wynn, M. (1989) The business benefits of PC office systems and end-user computing at Glaxo Pharmaceuticals 1984–1988, *Journal of Information Technology*, **4**, 1.

11 Hochstrasser, B. (1990) Evaluating IT investments. Matching techniques to project, *Journal of Information Technology*, **5**, 215–221.

Part Two

Part Two (Chapters 4–5) reports on current practice.

- **Chapter 4** describes the research project which showed how, in the companies we investigated, 16 projects were evaluated.
- **Chapter 5** presents several of the cases studies in the research in more detail. They illustrate the practical problems involved in evaluation and show that evaluation is inextricably linked to a series of other management issues.

4 How investments are evaluated in practice

Introduction

The process of appraising new investment is always a *political* process in so far as it touches on the diverse interests of many people and groups. Investment in new information system projects is no different in this respect – the introduction of a new system is an intervention at an organizational, as well as a technical, level.

This 'socio-technical' nature of information systems has two immediate consequences. First, in assessing the possible benefits and risks of a major new system the social impact must carry at least as much weight as the technical. Social impacts are pervasive and often intangible. They are at one and the same time very important and very difficult to quantify. Second, it is almost impossible to predict with any certainty how the intervention will play itself out and therefore to justify it properly at the outset.

Moreover, because the field of information systems is characterized by constant technological change, even though the problems are not new, there is no steady accumulation of experience or conventional wisdom to fall back on. There are few universally accepted guidelines for evaluating information system projects. There is no agreed language of accounting for information systems.

The result is something like a battlefield. There is a great deal of mud and smoke but very little by way of coherent strategy. The foot-soldiers make do and improvise with what is to hand. Some employ standard accounting techniques and forego much of the rich picture of social and technical change. A few attempt to move to higher ground, incorporating qualitative factors in various ingenious ways. Others give up entirely and proceed on the basis of an 'act of faith'.

Analysis of what practitioners do is nevertheless important. By comparing what is done across a range of organizations it becomes possible to identify the major issues and to tease out the salient features relevant to the problem of cost justification.

This chapter tells how the organizations we researched went about the problem. They provide lively illustrations but, like the case studies which follow in Chapter 5, they do not pretend to be fully researched results.

The chapter begins with a look at the context in which the decisions were made and at the level of change sought. This is followed by a summary of the differing procedures for performing an evaluation as they occurred in each organization. Following the discussions in the earlier chapters, particular issues raised are whether or not the justifications involved the quantification of intangible benefits and the timing of evaluations. Evaluations are done for many purposes and the timing of an evaluation will often reflect its purpose. Conversely the purpose may be determined by the timing.

The variety of people involved in the decision-making process is considered next. To help organize and generalize from the particular results of the research study, a framework has been borrowed from Gilbert *et al.*[1] This framework is a generic 'stakeholder' map, consisting of different groups of people who might be 'stakeholders' in an organization (Figure 4.4 below). Such frameworks are helpful in pointing beyond the question 'who was involved?' to 'who might have been involved?' By comparing the original map with what we found in our interviews, a new category of stakeholder is suggested – the 'external partner or collaborator'. This new category emphasizes the importance of new information and communication systems for defining and managing the boundaries of organizations.

Issues surrounding evaluation

Was there an IT strategy?

Current thinking in information systems theory takes it as axiomatic that IT investment should be made in the context of an IT strategy and that the IT strategy should act to support the overall strategic aims of the organization.[2] The research showed that theory and practice were different.

Fewer than half the organizations claimed to have an IT strategy (Figure 4.1) and only one spoke of IT in the total business context. Of those who did have a strategy, six covered the whole organization. Others were at subsidiary, divisional or departmental level. For the rest, IT investment decisions were made piecemeal.

What level of change was sought/expected?

In the course of discussing the key issues for business success in the 1990s, Michael Porter[3] suggests a hierarchy for IT impacts.

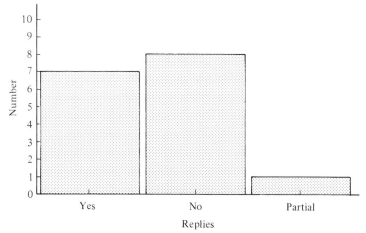

Figure 4.1 Is there an IT strategy?

The kinds of impact that were sought by the informants before the systems were installed were compared with Porter's 'levels' of hierarchy. The results are shown in Figure 4.2.

They show that the organizations were moving beyond using IT to automate activities in their current form. Instead they were planning to use the technology for enhancing and optimizing their activities. Five were using the networking capabilities of the systems to co-ordinate activities that were geographically spread.

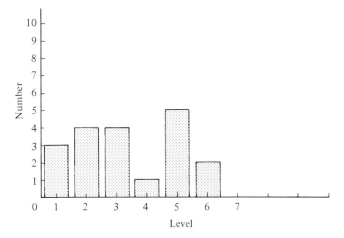

Figure 4.2 What level of change was sought? Level: 1, automation 3/16; 2, optimization 4/16; 3, enhanced functionality 4/16; 4, reconfigure work in new ways 1/16; 5, co-ordinate with activities that are geographically spread 5/16; 6, link to others inside and outside the firm 1/16; 7, shared activity 0/16

However, with one exception, they were not yet using the technology to reconfigure the way in which work was done, nor, again with two exceptions, were they using the systems to connect electronically with customers or anyone else *outside* the firm. None had considered using the technology to support co-operative work, although one or two organizations were edging towards this. For example, they had recognized that collaborative bids were made possible if everyone was using the same, or a compatible, technology. Few of the organizations had reached the levels of sophistication suggested in the literature, either in the way they considered IT or in the way they went about installing it and justifying its use.

Again, theory and practice were different.

What type of procedure was used? Was a justification required?

Although some sort of justification had been required in most cases, only about half had followed a standard justification procedure and only half required any quantification of the benefits. As a rule it was up to the champion to do whatever he or she thought was necessary to gain approval. Figure 4.3 gives an overview of the procedures.

Just nine out of the 16 projects were subject to a formal justification process. Of these, four were justified using classical ROI techniques.

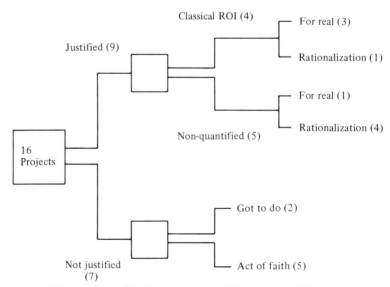

Figure 4.3 How the justification process and the context of the evaluation were handled

Three of these were 'for real'; the remaining one was clearly a rationalization of the decision which was taken on other grounds.

In five cases the justification was not quantified. Only one of these seemed to be 'for real' – as before, the others seemed to be rationalizations.

Of those that were not formally justified, two were justified as 'got-to-do' projects.

In the first of these cases the primary reason given was that the company's US-based clients were used to a better standard of presentation and service than obtained in the UK. The change had to be made if clients were not be to lost.

In the second the investment was considered an essential part of the IT strategy.

Five out of the seven were reported as being 'acts of faith'.

Was there an attempt at quantification?

Quantifiable, *tangible benefits* were identified in 10 out of the 16 projects. In the remaining six, even benefits which were tangible, and therefore might have been measured, were not attempted.

Only three of the 16 projects attempted to quantify *intangible benefits*. This did not mean that people were unaware of them. People seemed to be fully cognizant of intangible benefits. Rather, there was a general view that intangibles would not be acceptable as justification to those in authority.

However, in seven cases, intangibles were adduced as extra arguments to support the case for going ahead. In the remaining cases, intangible benefits were entirely excluded.

Often the justification procedure explicitly excluded anything but the most immediate operational benefits. In one case this was true even though there were much larger strategic benefits which might have been included (see Case Study 1 in Chapter 5).

In general, the focus was on short-term, quantifiable, tangible benefits. The larger picture was missing from the formal justifications.

At what stage(s) was the evaluation undertaken?

From the discussion in Chapter 2 it is clear that evaluation is not, or need not be, a one-off activity. Evaluation of information system projects may take place at many different points in the project lifetime. Rehearsing the stages identified in Chapter 2, the major points are:

- when strategy (reactive or proactive) is being developed
- when a specific project has been identified and the feasibility of the project is being assessed

- when the project is in the developmental stage
- when the system has to be 'signed off' (from developer to user) directly after implementation
- when the system is being monitored after implementation
- towards the end of the system's life: new options are being considered.

The research showed that justification, when it was done at all, was done at the 'feasibility' stage.

At first sight this is in contradistinction to the literature, which suggests that most evaluations are done at 'sign-off', i.e. when the systems are handed over from supplier to customer.[4] However, in this case it is probable that the differences were due to the nature of the projects being investigated. Virtually all of them were off-the-shelf systems, as opposed to tailor-made ones. For such systems the agreement to purchase is the key handover point from the supplier to the customer.

In addition six organizations undertook post-implementation audits. These were largely undertaken at the instigation of the vendor.

Speculating on the reasons for the apparent lack of enthusiasm for evaluation at other stages, one might suggest two factors. First, evaluation can be time-consuming and expensive whatever method is chosen. Post-implementation evaluation must itself be justifiable. Second, there is a tendency to regard information systems as 'sunk cost' and therefore to take no follow-up action.

We would argue against this view. We have already argued in principle that the impacts are unpredictable. We also found that in practice there was a marked difference between the expected outcomes and those which occurred. This point is illustrated in Chapter 5, most notably in Case Studies 1, 2 and 5. It follows that only an active benefits management policy will enable the benefits to be identified and exploited. Only an active policy will enable disbenefits to be controlled and risks to be minimized.

Who took part in the justification process? A stakeholder analysis?

The process of justifying investment in new information system projects involved a wide variety of people in each organization and, on occasion, outside it. To represent this variety two 'stakeholder maps' have been used. The first is a generic, high-level map including both internal and external stakeholders. The second is more detailed, in effect breaking open some of the boxes in the first map to reveal the internal stakeholder structure as found in the research.

A generic stakeholder map

A generic stakeholder map is provided by Gilbert *et al.*[1] and is reproduced in Figure 4.4. Of the groups depicted on the map, *employees* were, obviously, always involved. Somewhat less obviously, the *systems vendor* ('suppliers') was in many cases directly involved in the preparation of the justification. More than that, it was the vendor who was forcing the pace on post-installation audits. They saw the audits as part of the process of maintaining a relationship with the customer, ultimately as a way of developing the account.

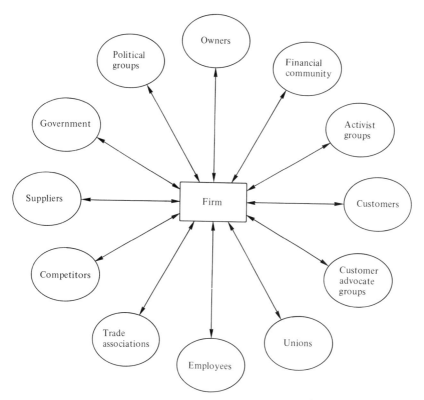

Figure 4.4 A stakeholder map of a large organization. (From Gilbert *et al.*, 1988)

None of the other groups on the diagram was directly involved.

Customers were not directly a part of the process, although customers' demands for compatibility with their own systems was often a decisive factor and although, in one case, customers were to be directly linked into the system. *Government* was only indirectly a party, in the weak sense that for several organizations the output of the system was required to conform to legal standards, thus putting a premium on certain configurations of system as opposed to others.

In one case government was itself the customer, imposing stringent electronic and hard-copy standards. These standards were in turn imposed as a result of agreements with a second government and had to hold across a range of collaborating suppliers.

The case suggests that the generic stakeholder map is in fact incomplete. There ought to be a stakeholder category of *external partners or collaborators*. Given the growth of EDI, and other networking applications which support collaborative work, it will be increasingly necessary to consult with people external to the firm as part of the justification and auditing processes.

An internal stakeholder map

Figure 4.5 shows the people or groups who had taken part in the decision process. The figure has been compiled from responses across all the organizations.

Not unexpectedly, most systems had relied heavily on a 'champion'; a specific person who had taken up the idea of the new system(s) and persuaded the organization that the investment would be worthwhile.

Of the champions, seven were managers, characteristically managers with a responsibility for administrative systems, six were 'systems', i.e. IS/IT people, and one was a user. In the remaining two cases the initiative came from a combination of a systems person and a manager (Figure 4.6).

Many of the cost justification procedures had involved *management at the most senior level*, including on occasion:

- the board of management
- the managing director
- the deputy managing director.

Other *general management* figures included:

- the group general manager
- the divisional director
- other managers in the group
- the head of department
- the departmental management team.

Included too were *financial management*:

- the director of finance
- a finance committee of the board of management

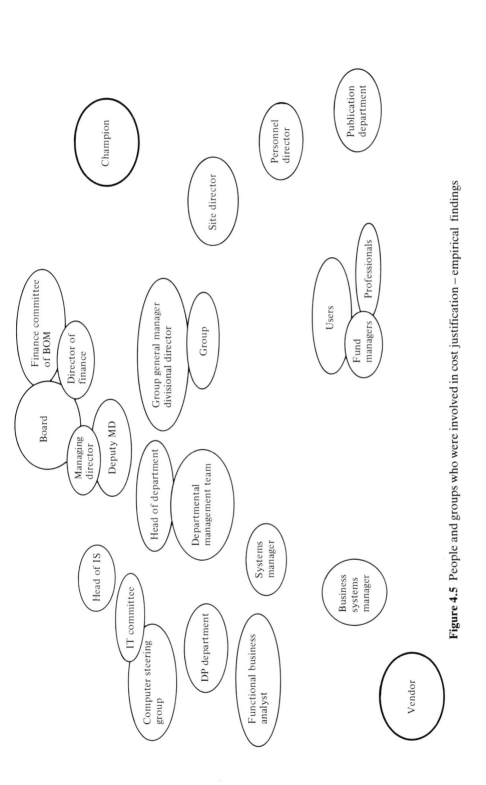

Figure 4.5 People and groups who were involved in cost justification – empirical findings

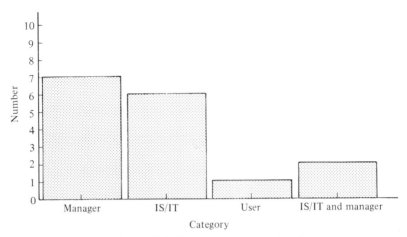

Figure 4.6 Who were the champions?

and *functional management*:

- the site director
- the publication department
- the (administrative) systems manager
- the business systems manager.

Information systems people mentioned included:

- the head of information systems
- an IT committee or computer steering group
- the data-processing department
- a functional business analyst. In this company the information systems department was devolved, so that systems analysts were situated in the user functions, for example in personnel.

Finally there were the *users*, including:

- support staff such as secretaries
- professionals, e.g. 'fund managers' or 'technical authors'.

A simple way to consolidate the list is to construct an 'internal stakeholder' map, generalizing from the empirical findings in Figure 4.5. On this evidence the consolidated map would look like that in Figure 4.7.

A more sophisticated approach would be to use an existing framework. Figure 4.8 shows the map of Figure 4.7 overlaid onto the Mintzberg framework we used in Chapter 3 to illuminate benefits. The resulting picture helps to address both the questions implicit in the

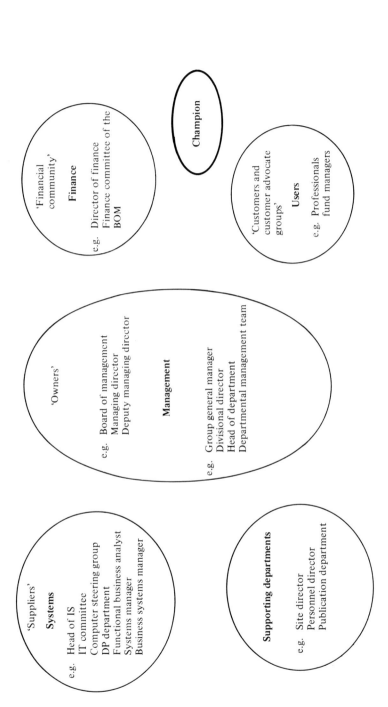

Figure 4.7 An internal stakeholder map

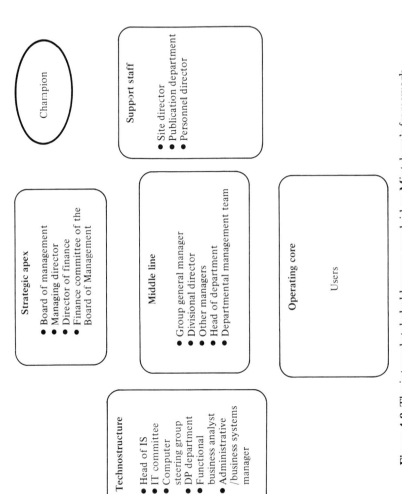

Champion

Support staff

- Site director
- Publication department
- Personnel director

Strategic apex

- Board of management
- Managing director
- Director of finance
- Finance committee of the Board of Management

Middle line

- Group general manager
- Divisional director
- Other managers
- Head of department
- Departmental management team

Operating core

Users

Technostructure

- Head of IS
- IT committee
- Computer steering group
- DP department
- Functional business analyst
- Administrative /business systems manager

Figure 4.8 The internal stakeholder map overlaid on Mintzberg's framework

definition at the head of this section: who are the 'holders' and what are their 'stakes'?

Mintzberg's frame provides a structure for the stretching question 'who might be involved?'; the empirical frame begins to answer the question. In practice, all parts of the organization are potentially involved. The empirical frame gives some idea, too, although it is by no means complete, of the structures within the larger categories.

The combination of the two re-emphasizes that different interests are involved, that different parts of the organization hold different stakes. As noted in the Introduction, a new information systems project is, inevitably, a political intervention.

Conclusions

The process of installing a system, from start to finish, confirmed a number of expectations; most systems had relied heavily on a 'champion' to the point where the project would not have gone ahead without their participation; very few attempts were made to treat the system differently from any other capital expenditure proposal; there was no consistency in the way in which cost justification had been approached; few organizations had carried out an *ex post* evaluation of the system except where initiated by the supplier of the system.

Moreover, the perception of what needed to be considered was disappointingly narrow, whether it concerned the possible scope and level of use of the system, the range of people who could or should have been involved or the timescale over which the evaluation could profitably have been undertaken.

Some explanation is needed. These people were not stupid, or insensitive to the social impact of new systems, or suffering from a lack of vision in other aspects of their work. Nor were they necessarily lacking in IT and information systems expertise.

A more appropriate explanation is that practitioners are in the front line. They have to find solutions that will pass muster. The champion has somehow to squeeze the enthusiasm, the doubts and the certainties into a form acceptable to the organization and this currently takes one of two forms: persuading the company to go along as an act of faith, or jumping through the hoops of a standard ROI assessment which may be appropriate, but more likely gives 'funny numbers'.

To sum up, management must evaluate processes which vary significantly from one situation to another in ways that are only partly understood. No single method will cope with this peculiarly complex problem, nor has any one method been accepted by the professionals as sufficient. That is why in the chapters which follow we suggest a *range* of methods – a small battery of weapons with which to attack the problem.

Notes and references

1 Gilbert, D. R., Hartman, E., Mauriel, J. J. and Freeman, R. E. (1988) *A Logic for Strategy*, Ballinger Publishing Company, Cambridge, Mass., p. 110 (quoting Freeman, R. E. (1984) *Strategic Management: A Stakeholder Approach*, Ballinger Publishing Company, Cambridge, Mass.).
2 Berenbaum, R. and Lincoln, T. J. (1990) Integrating information systems with the organisation, in *Managing Information Systems for Profit* (ed. T. J. Lincoln), Chapter 1, pp. 1–25, John Wiley and Sons, Chichester and New York.
3 Porter, M. F. (1988) *Business Success in the 1990s: What are the Key Issues?* Amdahl Executive Institute, London.
4 Kumar, K. (1990) Post-implementation evaluation of computer based IS current practice, *Communications of the ACM,* **33** (2), 203–212.
5 Mintzberg, H. (1983) *Structure in Fives: Designing Effective Organisations*, p. 11, Prentice Hall International Inc., London and Englewood Cliffs.

5 Case studies of evaluation in practice

Introduction

Any investigation of evaluation methods is likely to show just how closely and inevitably they are linked with a range of other organizational issues. The following case studies, selected from IT investments studied in our research, reveal what these issues are and how they are intertwined with the evaluation problem. The five case studies have been chosen because the systems involved are very similar and therefore differences in their planning, implementation and impact result from factors other than system differences.

Without consideration of these issues, the evaluation process at best can have its effectiveness reduced, and at worst be meaningless or even point in the wrong direction. Of course many other organizational procedures are acknowledged, at least privately, to be meaningless rituals, including non-IT capital expenditure procedures. However, even the biggest critics see them as being harmless or perhaps beneficial, but not in the way intended.

For example, ROI procedures may not, because of data problems, be accurate predictors of successful investments but they do at least provide a forum for the discussion of opportunity costs and alternative options. The risks in the IT area seem to be much greater: there is danger of an inadequate evaluation being misleading, bringing about wrong decisions or causing worthwhile initiatives to be rejected at an early stage.

IT seems to be different in two ways. First, it is now strategic, involving a wide range of benefits which are hard to quantify and handle. Second, IT is subject to rapid change. Although IT in some form has been around for centuries, the rapid changes mean that it always seems new. In addition, organizations have no great experience in dealing with it at the business rather than technological level.

Our research was designed to investigate the method of evaluation and not to pursue these other issues. However, the issues are of sufficient importance to warrant some attention. The case studies described below illustrate five issues but do not pretend to present fully researched results and conclusions.

In carrying out an evaluation of an IT investment there is a need for:

1 *A comprehensive search for benefits.*
Unexpected benefits are achieved, expected benefits are not. Contrary to popular opinion it is by no means obvious *ex ante* what can or cannot be achieved.

2 *A champion to drive the investment through.*
There can be scepticism about the value of IT investments, no doubt properly so in some cases. A real believer, not necessarily of high status, is needed to push against the obstacles which may be present even when the logic of the investment is sound.

3 *An understanding of related management processes.*
The evaluation of the investment may be of no use if the group carrying out the evaluation does not appreciate the whole investment decision-making process of which the evaluation forms a part.

4 *Good communications amongst stakeholders.*
Managers in different functions and at different levels may have very different perspectives on what the investment is meant to achieve and has achieved. Some simple publicity may be all that is needed.

5 *A post-implementation business evaluation.*
Surveys generally demonstrate that few organizations look at their systems to see whether they are achieving business benefits. They tend not to take steps to ensure that the planned-for returns on investment really happen. They are much more likely to check on technical performance.

These five issues are illustrated in the following five case studies.

Case Study 1: The need for a comprehensive search for benefits

The organization is a division of a worldwide pharmaceutical company. It develops, produces and markets products ranging from prescribed drugs through listed branded products to off-the-shelf medicaments for the UK and some Middle Eastern markets. Broadly speaking, manufacturing takes place in Wales; management, marketing and registration/licensing in the South East of England. Group Head Office, in the US, exercises fairly tight control over UK activities. In particular, headquarters dictates IT policy, setting computing standards and recommending the brands of equipment and software that can be bought.

One of the major tasks of the organization's medical department is creating the documentation for registering and licensing new drug products. This involves taking reports on:

(a) the 'recipe' of the product from the research and development groups
(b) the testing and trials of the product from the research and development groups
(c) quality assurance data from the manufacturing groups.

These and other reports are consolidated, bringing together text, tables, graphics etc. from the different parts of the company, into one document. This final report, which can run to thousands of pages, is sent to the relevant government department in London for approval. The drug cannot be sold until this department has registered and licensed it. The process is lengthy (it can take years) and usually involves discussions between civil servants and the company which result in changes to the documentation, requests for additional information and requirements for further research and testing. The process is therefore at the core of the organization's management.

The existing system was to produce as much documentation as possible on a series of stand-alone word processors and then cut and paste the rest. Medical department staff (qualified medical doctors) wrote reports in long-hand and gave them to secretaries working on the word processors.

The idea to change came from headquarters in the US, where advanced desk top publishing (DTP) systems had already been installed. These systems integrated the whole document production process and included facilities to produce sophisticated tables, charts, graphics etc. very easily. The UK president saw the result and brought the idea back to the UK, asking the management information systems department and the medical department to carry out a joint cost–benefit study. The system to be installed included workstations linked by an Ethernet to fileservers, laser printers and typewriters. The local network in the medical department in South East England was also linked to the manufacturing group in Wales.

The standard justification procedure which was stipulated by headquarters only allowed for quantifiable benefits. The resulting justification report had to be approved at four different levels of UK management before being forwarded to headquarters. Approval from the US was required since the capital requested exceeded £20 000, the maximum limit for approval in the UK. The justification was based on the achievement of four benefits:

1 Reduction in professional time estimated at 20%.
2 Reduction in clerical time estimated at 20%.

3 Further reduction in clerical time from templates for other formal documents.
4 Reduction in paper used.

This is not an exciting list. However, two more exciting benefits, known to the justifying team, were excluded from the report. They were:

1 Extra revenues through getting a product to market sooner, estimated at £5 million per day.
2 Easier approval by the ministry on account of improved presentational quality.

These benefits are greater in size and importance than the ones in the report. Why were they excluded? The reason was that corporate procedures and culture dictated that only hard, quantified benefits could be considered. The team felt that the inclusion of the 'exciting' but less tangible or measurable benefits would generate argument and delay because of the difficulties of providing precise quantification. They felt that the 'unexciting' benefits were sufficient by themselves to get approval.

So, the bigger benefits were omitted and the request was approved, with little opposition. An evaluation of the project after implementation revealed that the following benefits had been achieved:

1 It was thought that products had been got to market faster but since each product is unique it was not possible to prove this.
2 A doctors' data base has been created and linked to a 'phone in for information' facility. This has provided better service, leading to improved market share.
3 80% of medics (previously 0%) keyed in themselves. This shortened time and gave improved control.
4 The organization moved further down the management learning curve, making it easier to implement other applications.
5 The project has led to the creation of a data base of information required for registration in other countries. *But* paper usage was increased, not reduced.

The two most far-reaching and strategic benefits stemming from the project were therefore not included in the justification document: one (getting the project to market faster) for political reasons, the other (a new information product for doctors) because it was not foreseen. The outcome was a happy one – a successful project – but the situation does point to the need for management processes which can search for benefits and face up to their implications.

The real question is, however, what would have happened if the quantifiable benefits had not been sufficient to gain approval. Would the project have been delayed, losing valuable competitive advantage? Or would it not have gone ahead at all? Either would have been disastrous when the achieved benefits were so impressive.

Case Study 2: The need for a champion to drive the investment through

The organization is a firm of chartered accountants whose main business is carrying out financial audits. However, management consultancy has recently been added and this is expanding rapidly. There are offices in several locations, including London and Birmingham, but the head office is in Leeds.

The organization used to have a central computer department but because of its growing computer consultancy work, the department became a subsidiary. This group imposes policies relating to the choice of equipment and of software but it is still possible to make a case for bending the rules. At the time of investigation the policy was to standardize on personal computers (PCs). There was no long-term plan covering the development of IT usage within the company.

The administrative manager wanted a new system to produce the 3500 annual accounts (75% of the workload of her department), reports relating to consultancy (currently 20% of the workload but increasing) and other documents such as marketing material where high-quality output was required. The existing system was a series of stand-alone word processors which had been very successful but were limited in the range of functions they could tackle. They produced text only and accounts/tables had to be input as if text.

The process involved some tricky procedures for manipulating accounting documents and any new system would have to be able to handle them efficiently. It would also have to handle other tables and graphics and integrate them with text.

The IT committee (several partners plus IT experts from the computer group) agreed with the administrative manager that a new system was needed. However, they also wished to support the computer group policy of standardizing on PC systems for all functions throughout the firm. Accordingly the committee recommended that the administrative manager's department be upgraded to a PC system, allowing two years for the change to be made.

The administrative manager thought a PC system would be inadequate for the task since the software available at the time was not particularly suitable for producing accounts, or for improving presentational quality. She wanted some form of specialized DTP system.

The IT committee continued to press for PC standardization and that the Leeds headquarters should take the lead. The administrative manager continued to press the view that a PC system was not right for her department and that the inadequacy of a PC system would result in an explosion in staff numbers.

Eventually a subcommittee was set up to look into the issue. It took the views of a range of people and looked at alternative systems. A DTP system was brought in on trial on the grounds that its manufacturer was that of the existing successful system. This DTP system seemed to dominate others in terms of its ability to produce a table of information and of its user friendliness.

The administrative manager then produced a review document stating the reasons for acquiring the system. The subcommittee, especially the director of finance and the director of personnel, became the sponsor of the DTP system and recommended it to the senior committee of partners. The senior committee approved the DTP system. There is no question that if the administrative manager had not championed the system so persistently it would not have been bought.

Several months later the system was installed and comprised a network of workstations, fileservers and high-quality printers. It was used for tables (in accounts and also in reports which may run to over 100 pages and usually have many tables), graphics, maps and logos. Similar systems were eventually installed at other locations with the capability of communicating with the organization's other offices across the country.

The system also allowed the organization to transform the way it worked. The transformation stemmed from expediency. On budget day a report describing the implications has to be produced in time to be on clients' desks at 9 a.m. the next morning. All chartered accounting firms aim to be first on the grounds that a client will only read the first to arrive. The new system allowed this to be done more quickly and accurately. The text was input on workstations in London, the artwork and appendices in Leeds. There was continual swapping of files between Leeds and London until the complete document was ready. It was then transmitted to a variety of locations for printing.

The system achieved its cost reduction benefits but it also produced a large, unexpected benefit. The practice adopted for producing the budget report was spread to all types of work. Documentation was moved from one part of the country to another according to capacity available and costs. In the main this amounted to moving a lot of work from London with its high clerical staff costs to the North where costs and staff turnover were lower, and therefore quality higher. There is no doubt that the championship paid off.

Case Study 3: The need for an understanding of related management processes

The organization is a general technical consultancy company serving management and technical functions in many industries, of which the major ones are space and defence. It has a London-based service and support division, called 'X International', supporting functional divisions in different parts of the world.

An IT strategy was developed, part of which identified two requirements:

1 To make the production of documents, including consultants' reports, proposals, progress reports etc., more efficient and effective.
2 To improve inter-division communication, for information and documents, nationally and internationally, for the 3500 employees.

To meet the strategy a system which would meet these requirements worldwide was to be implemented. Development and implementation of this new system was driven by the managing director (MD) of X International who was also a main board director of the global organization.

The existing system for report production was based on a series of local word-processing centres. Consultants sent in long-hand documents which were returned in hard-copy form for proof-reading after typing. The graphics were prepared separately by hand by secretaries. There was a growing preference on the part of the consultants to key in their own material but there was very limited communication between the functional divisions. When it happened it was by telephone and fax.

To ensure an objective view, another consultancy company was employed to carry out a needs survey based on the strategy. This consultancy produced a report specifying the requirements and a list of major computer vendors was then invited to tender. Of those received, the response of one vendor was clearly the closest to the needs in terms of functionality although it was by no means the lowest priced. This vendor was then asked to prove in practice that its system would work satisfactorily. As a result managers attended demonstrations at the vendor's offices and some trial equipment was brought to X International.

The system did seem to be satisfactory for its applications, which included word-processing, graphics, communications within and between divisions, file storage, laser printing, data base management, table generation, business forms and spreadsheets. The MD of X International prepared a justification report for the main board in order to obtain final approval to purchase and implement the system.

The main board mainly comprised the MDs of the geographically based functional divisions. Unfortunately there was some opposition to the system at this level because some MDs objected to spending money from their own budgets. Their reasons were that if one of the major benefits was better communications then the equipment should be paid for centrally. X International's role is to advise rather than mandate and the final outcome was a recommendation that the linking equipment should be supplied to all subsidiaries and paid for centrally. However, the MDs would have to pay for the equipment installed within their own subsidiaries.

Given this agreement and the fact that opting out of the system would exclude a division from electronic mail, document exchange, corporate support for the system, training etc., it was thought that all the MDs would be persuaded to take it up.

When installed, a typical local network in a division comprised communications servers, printers and workstations. These local area networks (LANS) were joined together in a wide-area network linking offices in London with those elsewhere in Europe and the world.

The system achieved many of its objectives in terms of the expected benefits. It:

- enhanced the content of reports, giving clients a better product
- promoted the exchange of management information and other documents
- led to a consistent company style
- improved presentation, resulting in better service and, it was thought, more business
- gave exposure to advanced technology, taking the organization along the learning curve and making it easier to implement other systems
- improved job satisfaction for both consultants and clerical staff.

In spite of all this the system was, overall, a complete disaster. Only a third of the divisions opted in, the others keeping existing systems or adopting new systems which were incompatible. As a result the number of users never reached a critical mass and its facilities, particularly relating to communications such as electronic mail, were little used. Even some divisions that had opted in stopped using the system or indicated that leases would not be renewed when they ran out. Within three years the whole system had collapsed.

X International, the support group, had done many things according to the book: a business-related IT strategy had been developed, the requirements had been analysed objectively, users had been consulted, etc. The problem was that X International had misjudged the divisions and in particular had not understood the decision-making culture.

Interestingly, a formal audit of the system after it had collapsed, by a principal consultant of the organization, blamed the disaster on the computer vendor on the grounds of poor support. Certainly vendor support could have been better and the vendor did in fact reorganize as a result. It may even have been the 'last straw' for some of the subsidiaries that abandoned the system. But all this happened long after two thirds of the subsidiaries had already decided not to participate and vendor support could hardly have contributed to this.

Case Study 4: The need for good communications amongst stakeholders

The organization is part of a major aerospace group specializing in the design and production of military aircraft equipment. The contracting group is responsible for producing proposals, bids and tenders for the whole company. This involves liaising with the engineers doing the development work and the accountants doing the costing. It is the contracting group's overall responsibility to bring together formal proposals to be sent to client organizations, usually government departments in the UK and elsewhere. The group also has to liaise with other defence contractors in the UK and elsewhere with regard to the joint projects which are playing an increasing role in the defence industry.

The existing production system was based on a central clerical department with word processors for text. Graphics, scale plans etc. were produced manually by the draughting group under the supervision of engineers. The central clerical department used 'cut and paste' to incorporate them in the final documents, which were usually 300–500 pages in length with, on average, two pages of text to each diagram.

The move to a more up-to-date system originated when the manager of the contracting group saw a caravan display of computer-based office equipment in a local car park. He had not previously realized how rapidly office systems technology had improved. He felt that the latest equipment could offer substantial benefits in terms of project management and the production of technical documents. He quickly went to work to outline the type of system that would meet his requirements. The basic criteria were as follows:

1 A networked system was required, rather than a stand-alone.
2 He did not want to use the company's IBM mainframe; rather he wanted the group to have its own system so that he could retain control of the management of the system.
3 Nevertheless, the system had to be compatible with other company equipment, which included IBM and DEC mainframes and PCs of varying types. The latter were used for technical, engineering and financial work.

He contacted the vendor whose hardware he had seen in the caravan and the vendor lent some trial equipment for a month. Benchmarks were set, and passed within the month. The manager of the contracting group put together an investment proposal report and sent it to the board of directors, at the same time inviting them to come to see the trial system working. Some of them actually did so and enthusiasm was displayed at all levels. The report specified benefits in terms of cost, manpower and time savings.

Even so the decision process took six months. Eventually a network was installed comprising workstations, fileservers, printers and sophisticated software. The network was linked to other networks in the company.

Post-implementation, the system users were enthusiastic about an impressive array of benefits. The expected efficiency improvements had been achieved, including a massive reduction in the numbers of draughtsmen. In addition some unlooked-for benefits were mentioned:

- Deadlines were met more frequently.
- There had been a reduction in uncertainty and risk.
- Improved presentational quality was thought to have had an impact on bid acceptance.

The most interesting benefit was that the system had allowed the organization to take part in collaborative international proposals through the electronic exchange of information. What is interesting about this benefit was that while the *users* were aware that without the system the organization would have been barred from these international partnerships, not all *managers*, including some senior managers, were aware of this. The need for such a system had not been foreseen at a strategic level. Nor was this major benefit of its existence fully appreciated even after installation. In fact it was expertise in the use of the system which gave the organization a ticket to participate in the most lucrative business available, the large international collaborations.

Many senior managers thought of the system as a low-level cost reducer of minor importance. In fact it had strategic significance, but most managers were not aware that it had. Communication within the organization about the impact of the system was poor.

Case Study 5: The need for a post-implementation business evaluation

The asset management group at this organization manages investment portfolios for clients who range from pension funds to individual large investors and who are located in many areas of the world. At regular intervals reports on the performance of the portfolio are presented to the client. Other reports may be proposals to prospective new clients or recommendations for substantial changes in the structure of existing clients' portfolios. These reports are usually put together under extreme time pressures since the month end is the usual reporting date and clients would be suspicious of delays.

The existing system for producing reports was a network of word processors which produced text only. Graphics were produced by hand and integrated via cut and paste.

The motivation to change came from the director of asset management, who had a 'vision' of the importance of quality, in terms of both information and its presentation, in managing client relationships. There was also the generally recognized and perennial need to report on time. Not everyone in the organization saw the situation this way, many taking the view that only the performance of the portfolio had any business impact.

The debate was resolved by the group that dealt with US clients. They reported that the organization was well behind US rivals in reporting procedures and that business would be lost unless changes were made. Quite simply, the fund managers felt that their information-reporting and presentational style was not of the standard required throughout the US and business would be lost unless speedy action were taken. They suggested a system that they knew had been successful in the US.

No costed economic justification was put to the board. The decision about the system was taken on a 'got-to-do' basis. Since the fund managers who were complaining about the existing system were represented on the board there was no long decision process.

The original system was just three workstations. It was a success and other asset management groups soon asked for similar equipment. However, the additional equipment was subject to more critical justification than the original three workstations. A capital investment analysis was carried out and presented to the board.

There was some opposition from the central IT group, which objected to specialist systems that were not under its control. It preferred a PC option. However, it took the view that it should allow the asset management groups to go ahead and then say 'I told you so' when a disaster occurred.

The decision to buy the additional systems was straightforward since growing experience with the US group showed that the times to produce reports could be significantly reduced. In any case many fund managers had already promised clients tighter deadlines, or so they said. Consequently this decision also veered towards 'got to do'.

More workstations were installed in other areas. The local networks were linked together and eventually were linked in turn with the company's financial system, which held market information, including share prices and portfolio details. The system is used for producing integrated client reports which take financial data, tables and text from fund controllers' secretaries working on the financial network and add or improve tables and graphics under instructions from the fund controllers. Figure 5.1 illustrates the changes in working practices.

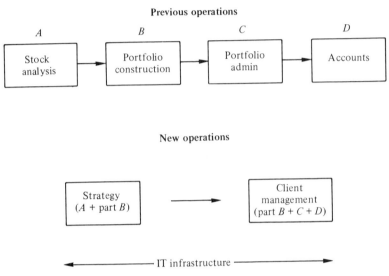

Figure 5.1 Changes in working practices for the financial services organization

The organization did not carry out a post-implementation review and had no intention of doing so until the computer vendor offered to undertake one free of charge. It produced some surprising results, both good and bad:

- Productivity improvements were far greater than anyone expected – the time to produce reports was reduced by 50–90%, depending upon the type of report.
- Customer service was enhanced. Fund managers now 'wouldn't dream of going to a meeting without a report'. Deadlines are (nearly) always met. Reports are more accurate: there are no transcription errors.
- Invoices showed that more computers had been bought than were in use: ten were found in a storeroom unopened in their boxes, to the surprise of the organization.
- Some UK clients asked to return to the old reporting style – with a price decrease.

Two dramatic changes brought about by the system did not require a post-implementation review to reveal them. First, the organization now never requires lengthy justifications for IT equipment, which has the same essential status as the telephone system. Second, the central IT group no longer exists. IT expertise is decentralized in all the business groups.

Surveys generally demonstrate that few organizations look at their systems to see whether they are achieving business benefits. They are much more likely to check on the technical performance. This case study suggests that surprising results might be revealed.

Conclusions

The chapter has highlighted five major factors contributing to the success or disaster of an IT investment:

1 A comprehensive search for benefits.
2 A champion to drive the investment through.
3 An understanding of related management processes.
4 Good communications amongst stakeholders.
5 A post-implementation business evaluation.

And there will certainly be more than five. All this points to the need for greater awareness of such catalysts. More than awareness, there is a clear need for an organization to make a significant effort to determine in advance what these factors may be in each particular case.

Part Three

Part Three (Chapters 6–8) sets out some of the options faced in terms of methods and techniques available to the evaluator.

- **Chapter 6** reports on some of the findings of the writers, consultants and researchers who have investigated the problem of evaluation in a variety of contexts.

Chapters 7 and 8 review and analyse some of the more interesting evaluation methods used in practice or advocated in the literature.

- **Chapter 7** focuses on methods which attempt to provide numerical measures of cost and benefit in order to support comparisons of one project with another and to help make the investment decision.
- **Chapter 8** emphasizes methods which are meant to explore the potential value of systems, taking into account the viewpoints of a variety of stakeholders.

6 Lessons from elsewhere

Introduction

> The ideas of economists and political philosophers, both when they are
> right and when they are wrong, are more powerful than is commonly
> understood. Indeed the world is ruled by little else. Practical men, who
> believe themselves to be quite exempt from any intellectual influences,
> are usually the slaves of some defunct economist. (John Maynard Keynes,
> *General Theory of Employment, Interest and Money*)

The evaluation of an information system, or for that matter of any
complex social system, rests on some or other idea of what 'evaluation'
is and why it is needed. 'Practical' approaches to evaluation often rest
on preconceptions which are deeply embedded, in much the same way
as Keynes observed for 'practical' approaches to economics. Often these
ideas are implied rather than fully expressed.

Nevertheless, because they are prior to the evaluation itself, the ideas
exert considerable influence over the way an evaluation is carried out
and on how the results are taken up. It is important to the smooth
running of an evaluation that they are made explicit and that evaluation
is not viewed in isolation, but integrated into other views of the
functioning of an organization.

The aim of this chapter is, therefore, to step back and explore
evaluation as an entity and, in so doing, to extend and broaden the view,
before moving on to the description of individual methods in the
chapters which follow.

The ideas which must be taken into account are not only ideas about
the nature and purpose of evaluation, but ideas about the nature and
purpose of information systems. They include ideas about what
measurement is, and when it is appropriate. Ultimately, they include
ideas about organization and work, about people and society (Figure
6.1).[1] Whilst it would be out of place to address too many of these
preconceptions in a book as narrowly focused as this one, it is both
necessary and helpful to expand on some of them – in particular those
preconceptions about measurement, evaluation and information systems of which we, the authors, are aware and which form the basis of

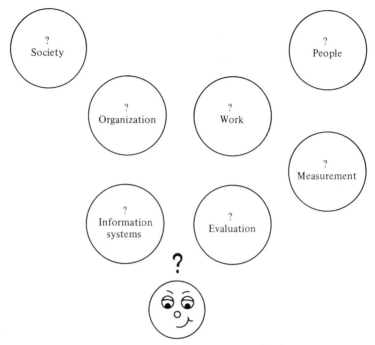

Figure 6.1 Ideas which influence evaluation

our approach. Specifically, we see information systems as social systems and the introduction of systems and their evaluation as social action.

The first part of the chapter brings together ideas from the theory of measurement, from other researchers in information systems and from researchers in other fields of social action. A visual representation is developed which helps to organize the different aspects of evaluation as social action. The representation is built up layer by layer and the result looks like nothing so much as an onion. Although not perhaps the most dignified of metaphors, the onion does convey something of the complexity of the problem.

The chapter goes on to look at work in other areas which call for the evaluation of social action. Many of the lessons are taken from evaluation studies carried out on social action programmes in the US in the 1970s. As our research has shown, these lessons are apparently having to be painfully re-learned today in the information systems community, 20 years later.

Measurement

Measurement is at the technical core of evaluation (and will be the core of the onion). Whatever the purpose of evaluation, it is likely that someone, somewhere will be trying to pin numbers on something. Grasping the fundamentals of measurement is therefore a necessary part of performing an evaluation.

Figure 6.2 shows a diagrammatic view of measurement.[2] It shows two ellipses connected by arrows. In the left-hand ellipse there are two

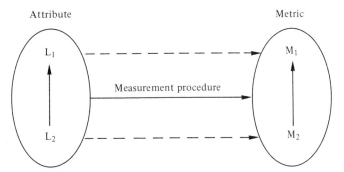

Figure 6.2 A simplified diagrammatic view of measurement

members of a collection of entities, L_1 and L_2, which have some attribute that is interesting to the person doing the measuring. For example, in a large organization operating at different sites, the personnel manager will want to know how many employees there are at each site. The entities are the sites and the number of people at each site is the attribute of interest. In the right-hand ellipse is a set of symbols (M_1 and M_2), commonly numbers, which also bear some relationship to each other. 20 is less than 40, for example. Measurement is an objective, empirical procedure which maps the attributes on the left to the numbers on the right in a way that preserves the relationship. So an effective procedure for measuring the number of people (counting them!) would map fewer personnel to a lower number, more personnel to a higher number.

The virtues of measurement are that the symbols are concise, precise and can be manipulated away from the original. One does not have to physically line up everyone in the company in order to calculate the total number.

Four aspects of measurement are important here.

Requisite variety[3]

The law of requisite variety states that if we want to design a control mechanism for a system then that control mechanism must be capable of measuring, evaluating and regulating all those attributes of the system that can have an impact on the performance of the system.

Failure to measure, evaluate or regulate any relevant attribute can cause the system to misbehave, possibly in an unpredictable manner.

The insights provided by the law of requisite variety can be applied to the problem of measurement as applied to the assessment of information systems. Any system of assessment which does not attempt to measure and evaluate all those aspects of the system under review which add value or add costs can result in misappraisals and suboptimal decisions.

Agreement about relationships

If some quality or attribute is to be measured, there needs to be agreement about the relationship in the left-hand ellipse. For instance, A 'is taller than' B, C 'is longer than' D are examples of relationships which people could be expected to agree on. Length and height are therefore measureable in principle. By contrast, A 'is more beautiful than' B, C 'is more charming than' D are not the sort of relationships about which one would expect universal agreement. Beauty and charm are not, in principle, measurable.

The range of attributes which are of interest in information systems evaluation includes concepts of different types with respect to measurement.

Some concepts, such as headcount reduction, are measurable, in principle if not always in practice. Others are not measurable even in principle. 'Presentational quality' is an example. Because people respond differently to different forms of information – some prefer words, others prefer pictures – it is impossible to obtain universal agreement on what constitutes an effective slide presentation.

Current usage refers only to these two types, measurable and unmeasurable and talks of only two kinds of impact, 'tangible' and 'intangible'. By going back to the theory we can refine the classification a bit further.

In between the attributes which can be taken as measurable and those which cannot are two groups of attributes. There are those, like 'cost', which may be measurable because there are powerful external rules and conventions which dictate that, although there is no universal understanding of the term, people will have some kind of understanding about what the numbers mean over a range of situations. There are others, like 'business success', which can perhaps be agreed within the confines of a limited number of people, although that agreement is not likely to hold very widely or even for very long.

Figure 6.3 shows the new classification. 'Tangible' includes attributes that are strictly measurable and those about which there is widespread agreement. 'Intangible' includes those which can be measured on the

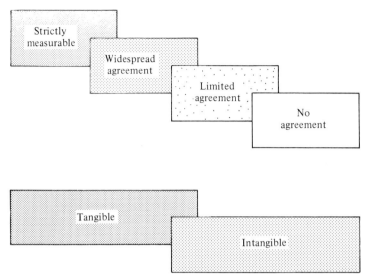

Figure 6.3 Classes of benefit with respect to measurement

back of limited agreement, for a short period, as well as those which are never going to be measurable. Clearly this is not a watertight classification. It does, though, make explicit the assumptions on which the ideas of 'tangible' and 'intangible' rest.

Procedure

To count as measurement, the procedure for mapping has to be empirical and objective. It is this question of procedure which is at the root of the arguments for and against different methods as described in the chapters which follow. Again, although some methods are objective, in the sense that anyone repeating the procedure would come to the same result, others are subjective, depending on individual reaction. Yet others can be seen to be mostly to do with the process of building a consensus, either about the relationship between attributes, the left-hand ellipse, or the measurement procedure.

Usefulness of the measures

The usefulness and validity of a measure depends on how well it fits with existing theory. The scales on which 'temperature' is measured, to take a common example, are acceptable because they fit with theory in physics, say, Boyle's law. Other measures of 'hotness' have been put forward in the past. They were not as useful and have fallen by the wayside. Similarly, measurements in information systems evaluation need to fit into some agreed management context in order to determine whether they are good measures or uninteresting ones.

Some caveats

In practice, single units of measure associated with information systems may be very difficult to find. It is difficult to reconcile the perceptions of a (large) number of people along a single dimension; the dimensions may themselves be difficult to articulate and, to represent a complex situation, there may have to be a number of dimensions along which the reconciliation has to take place. Also, although the unit of evaluation is often money, this may not always be the case. Rather, one may be talking about utility.

A social system perspective

In the evaluation of something as complex as a major information system, thinking about the method simply as a neutral procedure for evaluating a financial investment is too narrow a view.

First, the system itself, if it is sufficiently complex to warrant serious, possibly expensive attempts at evaluation, will have social and political goals as well as financial ones. All the goals must be taken into account if the results are to be understood.

For example, in one of the case studies which involved a public sector organization, the search for an improved system was prompted by discussions on the viability of the document production function. One strongly debated issue was whether the internal operation should be closed down and the work contracted out. At the same time it was recognized that technology had moved on and that, internally or externally, it would be possible to improve presentation whilst reducing costs. These were the formal reasons given. However, an additional spur for management was the desire to remove existing pressure for regrading through avoiding the need for typesetting. The system would de-skill this aspect of the work. The systems were thus brought in, at least in part, to change the balance of skills within the organization.

Second, evaluation is always done in a context and for a purpose: to prove a case, to justify an investment, to serve as the basis for a further decision. The results of an evaluation, even when they objectively obtain, hard, quantitative data, cannot be understood apart from the purpose for which they were obtained and the context of the decision to obtain them.

This context includes the many perspectives which are brought to evaluation by the different parties concerned. For example, in a previous study not part of the main research reported here, a saving due to a reduction in headcount was projected.[4] On the surface this was a measurable and tangible benefit and was used by the management team as part of the accounting for the project. In practice, however, the number was a contested part of a larger negotiation on manpower strength between management and trade unions. In this case the figure was really a bargaining chip, to be used as a threat, or to ease an accommodation on some other part of the deal. The number had a different significance for each side and its significance could not be appreciated outside the organizational context. The introduction of the new system, and the way in which it was evaluated, could be better understood if they were seen as social action, rather than as 'straightforward' investment evaluation.

Content, context and process

A useful way to think about evaluation-in-context has been suggested by Pettigrew and taken up by Symons.[5] They make a distinction between the content of an evaluation, i.e. what is measured, the context in which the evaluation takes place and the process of evaluation, which is seen as a social process.

These three perspectives are shown in Figure 6.4, overlaid on the measurement diagram. They define the layers of interest in evaluation: the 'rings' of the 'onion'.

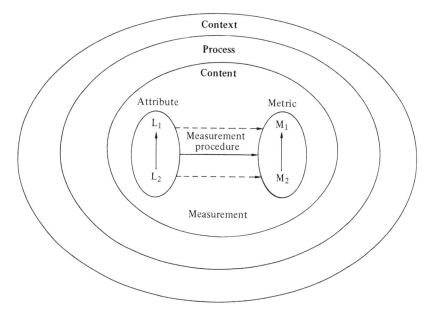

Figure 6.4 The content–process–context rings of the evaluation 'onion'

In the first ring, evaluation is seen as content. From this perspective evaluation is concerned with identifying costs and benefits and balancing the two. The important problems, *ex ante*, from this perspective are those of estimation. *Ex post* they are cause and effect. In both cases one needs to ask what is to be included? How is it to be measured?

The second layer is about the process of evaluation. In this ring not only the results of the evaluation, but the way in which it is carried out, its social role and how it plays itself out over time are placed in the foreground. It is, as it were , the 'meta-evaluation', a view on whether or not the evaluation was successful and the impact of performing the evaluation.

Recognizing evaluation as both content and context adds a third ring and generates a whole new range of questions: Who was involved? What did they do? Were they concerned to quantify the results? What level of change were they aiming at? Were there conflicting aims or interests? When was the evaluation carried out? Why was it carried out? What did that suggest about the purpose of the evaluation? What else was happening at the time? The very heavy emphasis which we have placed on this ring, both in the research and in the way we have described and interpreted its results, reveals very clearly our own models of what evaluation is, or ought to be about. In our experience, this context layer is essential to the understanding of what is actually happening. At times, as is evidenced by the number of systems that were justified by a 'back-door' route, the context entirely overwhelms the content.

The significance of the second, intervening layer, is that it draws attention to evaluation as a (group) learning process, mediating between content and context. Evaluation is one way, among many, in which people in organizations make sense of their environments, bargain and negotiate together to form a new consensus. In the process they adjust their mental models of the business and the place of information systems within it. In Symons's view, this 'learning' function of evaluation is critical during the development and implementation of a new system, when evaluation has both a learning and a control function.

In the 'onion' model, there are at least two key areas where this coming together to form a new, consensual view is critical. First, in the measurement 'core', agreement is required on the relationships between attributes of interest before measurement can be said to be have any meaning. Some common scale of 'goodness' or 'badness' has to be developed in the minds of the people who are involved. Second, in the content layer, there needs to be agreement on what is to be measured and what the procedure will be. Both of these will be affected by what is happening in the context layer, in other words by the social processes that surround the evaluation proper. And both serve to change the mental models of the people concerned. The importance of including the middle layer is to make this learning process visible and conscious and, where possible, to direct it to the organization's advantage.

A social action perspective

So far, we have used the term 'social action' intuitively, without defining it too closely. There is, though, a paper by Lyytinen *et al.*[6] which takes an existing formal theory of 'social action' (as proposed by Jurgen Habermas) and uses it to construct a framework for better understanding information systems.

Lyytinen and his colleagues use the formal theory to suggest four types of social action:

- instrumental
- strategic
- communicative
- discursive.

Instrumental action builds on a view of systems, both organizational systems and technical systems, as tools. As the authors have it, 'human qualities are ignored'. Clearly such a view is only valid when the systems are:

(a) not social, i.e. natural or technical, or
(b) when there is sufficient agreement about the attributes of a system to make them, effectively, objective.

In either of these cases, the problems of evaluation are problems of measurement and estimation and especially of measurement procedure. They are problems of what to measure and how to measure it, i.e. they fit into the first, 'content', ring of the onion.

Strategic action, as the name implies, is action taken in furtherance of individual, or group, interests. Other actors in the system are assumed to be doing the same thing, i.e. acting in furtherance of their own interests. There are possibilities for conflict, and for co-operation. 'An actor must cope with both co-operative and conflicting interest situations and find the best strategy to pursue their self-interest.' Strategic action is essentially action in the outer, 'context', ring of the onion.

Communicative action is directed towards achieving consensus, agreement or understanding. It straddles all three rings. As we have seen, agreement is required in the measurement core, especially as to the nature of the relationships between entities or attributes that are going to be measured. Agreement is required as to what is to be measured and how. Communicative action underpins the context ring. Mutual understanding is required if any kind of group learning is to take place.

Discursive action takes place when understanding cannot be 'taken for granted', when the very terms in which matters are discussed are themselves subject to agreement. Like communicative action, discursive action takes place in all three rings.

Looking at the measurement core first, measurement is itself discursive action. It gives a very precise meaning to terms. For example, the quantification processes necessary in a cost–benefit analysis define, often to the level of a single number, the meaning of each 'cost' and 'benefit'.

In the context ring, discursive action is necessary in resolving problems which occur when communication breaks down.

Discursive action is perhaps most critical in the middle, process ring. Learning, individual learning, but also organizational learning, is very much a matter of settling on and understanding the terms in which conversation is carried out. Think of the technicalities of almost any subject and how much is simply a matter of understanding what is meant by the 'jargon'. Think how much easier it is to communicate within a team that has developed a common vocabulary. The process of evaluation, when viewed as a learning process, can be used as an opportunity for developing such a common vocabulary, so that communication can be, as Lyytinen and his colleagues have put it, 'clear, direct and appropriate to the situation'.

Lessons from the evaluation of social action programmes

Large-scale, broadly aimed social programmes, such as the Headstart programme in education, were established in the US during the period 1960–1970. Evaluating these programmes proved to be extremely problematic and became a major subject of research in its own right. The problem areas and the stories which are told would not be out of place in the current discussion in information systems.[7] There are descriptions of 'bureaucratic' problems, for example, which came about because people did not like being evaluated and acted to obstruct the evaluation. Other accounts tell of 'pseudo-evaluations' which were designed to prove a political point.

The research identified five problem areas in evaluation research:[8]

- conceptual problems
- methodological problems
- bureaucratic problems
- political problems
- organizational problems.

These categories fit closely within the inner rings we have already identified. Conceptual problems are prominent in the measurement core and in the content ring. Methodological problems fall clearly in the content ring. Bureaucratic, organizational and political problems are problems of context. Notably, though, the middle layer is missing; that is, the use of evaluation as itself an occasion for learning is not specifically singled out.

Putting it all together

The 'onion' is now complete (Figure 6.5). We can summarize as follows.

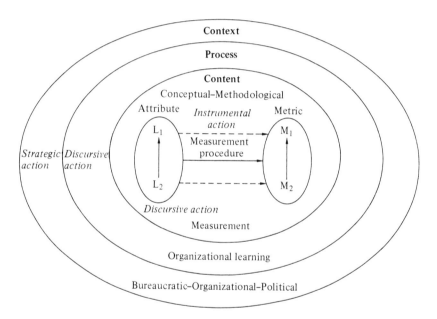

Figure 6.5 The evaluation 'onion'

Measurement is at the core of evaluation. In the context of evaluation, obtaining valid measurements depends in the first instance on getting agreement as to the nature of what is to be measured; specifically agreement on what constitutes 'more' or 'less' of it. Action in the measurement core is primarily discursive. Tackling questions of 'what and how' to measure is valid only if the discursive action is successful, i.e. if there is prior agreement on concepts.

The inner (proper) ring is *content*. The primary question is 'what' and problems are methodological, revolving around technical measurement issues of estimation and measurement procedure – what and how?

Human, social issues are not so much absent or irrelevant, but assumed away. Action is instrumental or discursive.

The outer ring is *context*. Here the primary questions are 'who?', 'when?' and 'why?'. Problems revolve around questions of intention: 'what are/were people trying to do?', 'what stake do/did they have in the outcomes?' Psychosocial issues are to the forefront, as are bureaucratic, organizational and political problems; little can be assumed and the logic of evaluation is rooted in the situation. Action is strategic and communicative. Self-interest is acknowledged.

The third, middle ring, is *process*. In this perspective it is the very act of evaluation that is the focus of attention, together with the effect it may have on learning and understanding as the process unfolds. Action is communicative and discursive. The salient impacts are on mutual understanding, on the development of a common language. Proper attention to this ring allows the learning aspect of evaluation to be recognized and managed for the benefit of the organization.

Practical issues surrounding an evaluation

Evaluation is an essentially practical affair. It requires organization. As the description of different methods in the chapters which follow will show, each method implies a way of proceeding; sometimes, as for example with multi-objective, multi-criteria methods (Chapter 9), the procedure is the most outstanding feature of the method. Experience has shown, however, that beyond the method proper there are better and worse ways of carrying through an evaluation and that the likelihood of a successful evaluation can be increased significantly through careful attention to organization and presentation.

What follows is an evaluation 'checklist'. It represents 'good practice' selected from the literature, both the information systems literature and the writing on social action evaluation referred to earlier in the chapter.[9] Included, too, are suggestions from our own research. These embrace both advice passed on by the interviewees and suggestions we would make having observed the pitfalls which beset such evaluations as were undertaken. The checklist has not been tested; it is presented simply as an amalgam of experience which may be helpful in considering what needs to be done and the practical issues that might arise. It is addressed primarily to people who will perform the evaluation; those who, when asked to evaluate a new system, have to answer the question 'What do I *do*?'

Following the scheme in the earlier part of the chapter, the questions are classified as (primarily) content, context and process.

Table 6.1 An evaluation checklist: summary

---

1 Is there a description of the problem?
2 What are the background and context?
3 How does the assessment relate to other decision-making in the organization?
4 What resources are available?
5 Who are the 'stakeholders'?
    Who is the commissioning client, the 'sponsor', and in what role are they acting?
    Who is the 'champion'?
    Who will carry out the evaluation?
    What are their aims?
    Who are the people or groups targeted by the new system?
    Who will be impacted by the new systems?
    Who is directly impacted?
    Who is indirectly impacted?
6 What values have to be taken into account, for example: organizational values, professional standards?
  What or who is the source of these values?
  What approach to evaluation will be taken?
7 Has the process been carefully defined and communicated? Is the discussion framed in terms that can be understood by everyone concerned?
8 Will the results of the evaluation be generalizable, exportable to other similar situations?
9 How significant will the results be?
10 How will the results be reported; including timing, presentation, media, format?
11 Who will present the results/report?
12 What recommendations for improvement are being made as a result from the evaluation?
  What (management) action follows the evaluation?
  Is there a provision for evaluating the evaluation?

---

1 Is there a description of the problem? (content)

It is always helpful to have a working definition of what problem precisely the evaluation is supposed to solve. What is perhaps not so obvious is that this description will change as the evaluation proceeds and that there needs to be a mechanism for agreeing and updating the original. For one thing, as has been noted above, the evaluation process can be made into an opportunity for learning so that the understanding of the problems gets deeper as time goes on. It is surely useful to incorporate this newer understanding into the problem definition, rather than to stick rigidly to the original formulation. Moreover:

> The description with which we begin the iterative cycles through the checklist is the client's description; but what we finish up with will be the evaluator's description, and it must be based, if possible, on discussions with consumers, staff, audiences and other stakeholders.[10]

To this one should add a warning, sounded clearly by Lincoln and Shorrock,[11] about the dangers of working with confused objectives, inconsistent objectives and hidden agendas. Evaluations serve many purposes, not least the purposes of the evaluators and those who commission them. A sensible rule would be to ask 'Is the purpose of this evaluation to improve something? Or to prove something?' Only the former is likely to command the confidence of all stakeholders. The latter ought to carry a health warning.

2 What are the background and context? (context)

A full description should include a description of the key political and economic pressures faced by the organization as seen by the evaluator. In the language of the previous section, this will be an account of the 'context layer'.

One particular question here is whether or not the system can be considered apart from the organizational background and other changes which are happening at the same time. It may be very difficult, even wrong, to attribute value to the system *qua* system, especially if the introduction of the system takes place alongside or as a part of other major changes.

3 How does the assessment relate to other decision-making in the organization? (context)

Information systems are only one kind of investment made by an organization. Information systems investment may need to be compared with other opportunities for investment. Such comparisons must be made on a 'level playing field', using the same or clearly comparable methods.

Moreover, organizations cannot change their spots easily. An organization which traditionally uses very formal methods for cost justification elsewhere cannot be expected suddenly to throw caution to the winds in pursuit of a 'soft' method. Where the evaluator nevertheless deems it necessary to take on board 'soft', 'qualitative', 'intangible' outcomes, and it will be obvious from what we have written that we are ourselves convinced of the importance of such outcomes, a considerable programme of persuasion and confidence-building may be required as part of the evaluation process. As has been noted in the first part of this chapter, this will involve communicative action, directed towards achieving the acceptability of the evaluation, as well as discursive action to build understanding of the terms in which matters are discussed.

The way in which the chosen method goes with the grain of the organizational culture is one of the most important criteria by which a method has to be selected.

4 What resources are available? (context)

Different methods of evaluation imply different levels of cost. The method chosen will have to reflect the cost constraint (see also the discussion of individual methods in Chapters 7 and 8 and the discussion in Chapter 11 on selecting a method).

5 Who are the 'stakeholders'? (context)

Identification of stakeholders and their stakes is crucial both to the success of a project and to the acceptance of its evaluation. The research identified numerous individual stakeholders and stakeholder groups, as reported in Chapter 4. In this section we rehearse some of those stakeholder types, and add more, basing the additions primarily on the experience of the evaluation of social action programmes.

Who is the commissioning client, the 'sponsor', and in what role are they acting? Who is the 'champion'?

Two people are likely to figure prominently in any evaluation: the sponsor and the champion. The sponsor is the person who pays. The champion is the person who will drive (or has driven) the project. Both have an investment and a vested interest in the project. They may, on occasion, be the same person. The practical importance of identifying each is two-fold.

First, there is a question of communication. If the sponsor is, for example, the chief executive, then the evaluation needs to be framed in terms which he or she finds significant, like value for money and links to corporate strategy. Jargon-filled descriptions of the value of the system in terms of 'mips' and 'bytes' will not do.

Second, there is a question of loyalty. It is an ethical question. The interests of the sponsor are not always aligned with the interest of the organization as a whole. For example, in one case study of an industrial firm, the system had been deliberately chosen by the head of department to be *incompatible* with the company systems, in order to preserve his independence from the information systems group. An evaluator hired by the department head would have to decide where his or her loyalties lay as the evaluation would be different in each case.

Who will carry out the evaluation?

What are their aims? What stake do they have in the outcome of the (new) system? In the outcome of the evaluation?

Gregory and Jackson[12] make a telling point when they describe the people most directly concerned with the evaluation as the 'evaluation party'. Not only do they remind us that it is necessary to identify who, precisely, is going to be involved in the evaluation, but they also remind us that any people chosen will bring a unique perspective to the evaluation, both as individuals and as a group. They are likely to form a fairly small group which has a dynamic of its own.

The role of the evaluation party needs to be clearly defined with regard to the rest of the organization. For example, will it be their function to set performance targets? Will they act as policemen with regard to those targets? Or will they act to advise, help and counsel, to prove or to improve? Evaluation requires trust and co-operation from the people who are being evaluated and they need to know precisely what they are letting themselves in for if they agree to co-operate.

Who are the people or groups targeted by the (new) system and who will be impacted by the (new) systems?

The point here is to distinguish the two. For example, in a DTP company, producing highly technical documentation, the introduction of a new system was directly aimed at the authors. However, as the authors took on more responsibility for their own basic typing, the company's secretaries found that their role was changing too. They were able to concentrate more on the creative side of page layout and design, and less on basic inputting.

Who is directly impacted and who is indirectly impacted?

Again, the point is the distinction between the two groups. In considering impact, it is important to remember groups external to the company, e.g. customers, regulators and suppliers, who will all be indirectly impacted by a change in the system.

6 What values have to be taken into account, e.g. organizational values, professional standards?

What or who is the source of these values? (context) and what approach to evaluation will be taken? (context and process)

The point has been made above that unless an evaluation takes on board the fundamental values of an organization, it is likely to be dismissed as 'counter-cultural'. This is not to argue that company values must never be challenged. Rather, it is to say that there has to be a managed process of change and a new consensus formed.

There are, too, the perspectives of the evaluating party to be taken into account. If the evaluation party is itself of one mind, and that is to take a very objective, 'hard-nosed' view, trying to impose a 'soft' approach will be met with resistance. On the other hand, if there is a variety of approaches present in the evaluation party, approaches which foster consensus, even very 'soft' approaches, will be appropriate and acceptable.

7 Has the process been carefully defined and communicated? Is the discussion framed in terms that can be understood by everyone concerned? (context and process)

Case Study 5 (Chapter 5) shows the need for good communications among managers if the true impact of the system is to be appraised.

8 Will the results of the evaluation be generalizable, exportable to other similar situations? (content)

This may or may not be an important criterion, depending on the frequency with which the exercise is to be carried out.

9 How significant will the results be? (context)

Clearly the time, effort and resources put into an evaluation must reflect the importance, or otherwise, of the results. For example, although there is in general a strong case for post-implementation audits, if no management action will be taken as a result, there is no reason to do the audit.

10 How will the results be reported; including timing, presentation, media, format? (content and context)

As noted above, there are different audiences for the results of a justification. Each needs to receive the results in a suitable format. The responsibility for this lies with the evaluator/evaluation party.

11 Who will present the results/report? (context)

The question of presentation of the results is political. Broadly, the status of the presenter should match that of the recipient. Ideally, the evaluation party will reflect the structure of the client.

12 What recommendations for improvement are being made as a result of the evaluation? (content)

What (management) action follows the evaluation? (context) and is there a provision for evaluating the evaluation and taking on board the lessons that have been learned? (process).

Conclusion

Evaluation is not a neutral or an innocent activity. Rather, it rests on a number of underlying beliefs, including beliefs about the nature of evaluation and about information systems. Drawing on the work of other researchers, most particularly in the fields of measurement, information systems and social action research, this chapter has presented a view of the issues surrounding the activity of evaluation *per se*. From them we see that:

- Evaluation is a multi-layered activity, including: content – that which is being measured; process – the way in which it is carried through; and context – the complex organizational (or even inter-organizational) situation in which it must be done.
- The process by which evaluation is carried out can present an opportunity for organizational learning and improved communication – or not!
- Evaluation is a sensitive activity. Careful thought needs to be given early on to practical issues such as the composition of the 'evaluation party' and its relationship to other stakeholders as well as to presentation and communication. Because evaluation tends to be an iterative process these questions do not disappear, but need monitoring all the way through.

Notes and references

1 A convincing demonstration of the advantages of taking an explicit view of models of organization is given by: Morgan, G. (1986) *Images of Organisation*, SAGE, London. Morgan describes eight images of organization and the kind of insight that each provides, and shows how to meld these insights together to produce a rich description of the organization.
2 This view of measurement is taken from the work of Ludwik Finkelstein. See, for example, Finkelstein, L. (1975) Fundamental concepts of measurement definition and scales, *Measurement and Control*, **8**, 105–111. A discussion of measurement in the context of information systems is to be found in: Stamper, R. (1973) *Information in Business and Administrative Systems*, B. T. Batsford, London.
3 The notion of requisite variety emerged from theoretical concerns about viable control systems developed within the discipline of cybernetics. Its inventor was Ross Ashby, who wrote: Ashby, R. (1959) *An Introduction to Cybernetics*, Wiley and Sons, Chichester. A good account of the notion is also provided by: Conant, R. C. and Ashby, W. R. (1970) Every good regulator of a system must be a model of that system, *International Journal of Systems Sciences*, **1**, No. 2.
4 Farbey, B., Avgerou, C., Cornford, A., Land, F. and Piachaud, D. (1988) *Information Systems. Information Technology: The Case of the DHSS*, Internal Report, London School of Economics, London.

5 Symons, V. (1990) Evaluation of information systems: IS development in the processing company, *Journal of Information Technology*, **5**, 194–204; Symons, V. and Walsham, G. (1991) The evaluation of information systems: a critique, in *The Economics of Information Systems and Software* (ed. R. Veryard), pp. 70–88, Butterworth-Heinemann, Oxford; Pettigrew, A. (1987) Context and action in the transformation of the firm, *Journal of Management Studies*, **24** (6), 649–650; Pettigrew, A. (1985) Contextualist research and the study of organisational change processes, in *Research Methods in Information Systems* (eds E. Mumford, R. Hirschheim, G. Fitzgerald and T. Wood-Harper), Amsterdam, pp. 53–78. Symons' case study provides a salutary account of the history of a project and its evaluation. She writes, 'Evaluation is poorly developed not because it lacks importance or relevance but because it is *sensitive* as well as difficult.' (Our emphasis.)

6 Lyytinen, K., Klein, H. and Hirschheim, R. (1991) The effectiveness of office information systems: a social action perspective, *Journal of Information Systems*, **1**, 41–60.

7 Two books containing comprehensive discussions of the issues are: Madaus, G. F., Scriven, M. and Stufflebeam, D. L. (1983) *Evaluation Models: Viewpoints on Educational and Human Services Evaluation*, Kluwer-Nijhoff Publishing, Boston and The Hague; Rossi, P. H. and Williams, W. (eds) (1972) *Evaluating Social Programs: Theory, Practice and Politics*, Seminar Press, New York and London.

8 Rossi, P. H. and Williams, W. (eds) (1972) *Evaluating Social Programs: Theory, Practice and Politics*, Seminar Press, New York and London.

9 Most of these questions are taken from: Madaus, G. F., Scriven, M. and Stufflebeam, D. L. (1983) *Evaluation Models: Viewpoints on Educational and Human Services Evaluation*, Kluwer-Nijhoff Publishing, Boston and The Hague.

10 Madaus, G. F., Scriven, M. and Stufflebeam, D. L. (1983) *Evaluation Models: Viewpoints on Educational and Human Services Evaluation*, Kluwer-Nijhoff Publishing, Boston and The Hague.

11 Lincoln, T. J. and Shorrock, D. (1990) Cost justifying current use of information technology, in *Managing Information Systems for Profit* (ed. T. Lincoln), John Wiley and Sons, Chichester, pp. 29–42.

12 Gregory, A. J. and Jackson, M. C. (1992) Evaluation methodologies. A system for use, *Journal of the Operational Research Society*, **43**, 19–28.

7 Evaluation methods: quantification and comparison

Introduction

In Chapters 4 and 5 we described how evaluation was carried out in practice by a number of companies. Chapters 7 and 8 describe some of the many evaluation and decision-aiding techniques described in the literature, some of which are also used in practice. However, surveys have shown that most organizations use variants of a small part of the range of methods available, and that many organizations employ an *ad hoc* approach to evaluation, often inventing a method to suit a particular situation. In a sense many managers 'pick and mix' from the wide range of available methods. The chapters are not intended to provide a catalogue of all available methods. We have selected methods which are widely used in practice and others which we believe will be of interest both to practitioners and researchers.

There are two principal processes which together make up evaluation: data collection and decision-making. The first is concerned with establishing the costs and benefits of the system under consideration. In *ex ante* evaluation the evaluation problem hinges on the need to estimate future costs and benefits. In *ex post* evaluation the problem is to identify costs incurred and benefits achieved and to determine the extent to which these were the outcome of the changes under consideration. Each method is supported by a set of processes designed to define and agree the objectives of the change and to collect data on costs and benefits.

Data collection methods include organization and methods (O&M) practices, work measurement, costing methods, operational research (OR) methods, including model building and simulation, the use of spreadsheet techniques, cost estimation techniques such a the Constructive Cost Model (COCOMO) and function point analysis.[1] Methods which help to identify objectives and achieve consensus and commitment include strength, weakness, opportunities and threat (SWOT) analysis, the identification of critical success factors, Delphi methods, decision conferencing, variance analysis[2] and strategic modelling using methods derived from industrial dynamics.

The second aspect is concerned with decisions which justify going ahead with the project (*ex ante*) or which provide retrospective justification that the project had indeed been worthwhile (*ex post*). The two aspects can be separated in that a data collection method provides input into the decision model, but many data collection methods include the decision-making component within the method.

In Chapters 7 and 8 we emphasize the characteristics of each of the selected methods but do not go into the detail of how the method is used. However, attention is drawn to the relevant literature so that readers who want to explore the methods in more detail can get the help they need.

All methods can be analysed with respect to a number of important characteristics:

Complexity

Methods vary considerably in their complexity. Some methods require a large amount of data and some of the data are themselves difficult to identify and collect. Other methods are conceptually difficult to understand or require a great deal of expertise and experience to use properly. Some methods require considerable resources – perhaps the time of senior management – to be used successfully.

Ease of communication

Methods vary in the ease with which they can be learned and how well they can be understood both by decision makers and those who have to be persuaded that a correct decision has been reached.

Degree of precision and quantification

While some methods attempt to predict cash flows for tangible net benefits over time, other methods provide ballpark estimates or rough and ready guides. Some methods attempt to provide exact numerical values on which to base decisions, while others provide a ranking of alternatives but no precise quantification. Some methods only value directly attributable costs and benefits, while others provide some measure of intangibles. Whilst some methods rely on collecting data to obtain numerical results – e.g. cash flows – other methods tend to stress the process by which results are arrived at.

Facilities provided by the method

Methods vary considerably in the facilities they offer the evaluator. Some methods incorporate facilities for analysing the robustness and sensitivity of the answers yielded by the methods. A few provide explicit ways of assessing the risk of the project under review. Some methods attempt to cope with uncertainty by the use of best and worse case analysis, and others provide 'what if' capabilities for the evaluation of alternative scenarios. Some methods provide the analyst with computer support to facilitate the evaluation. Some methods are based on hard systems thinking, and others incorporate techniques derived from the soft systems movement. Some methods permit comparison of the returns from IT projects with returns from other projects, including non-IT projects.

Congruency with established IT methodologies

Some methods are part of or are congruent with established requirements analysis or other IT methodologies. Thus some methods incorporate value chain analysis or make use of critical success factor analysis. If the development method provides the data needed by the preferred evaluation technique, as a natural byproduct of its mode of working, much effort may be saved and the problems of communication and understanding between developers and evaluators will be eased.

Extent of senior management involvement

Some methods are designed to be used only by technical personnel from the accounting or the IT function, while others permit the involvement of senior management.

In Chapters 7 and 8 the methods are roughly grouped as follows:

Chapter 7 concentrates on methods which aim to provide precise quantification of costs and benefits, and methods which permit decision takers to compare the costs and benefits of different system designs or to compare the project in question with other projects which compete for investment capital. Such methods tend to rely on conventional accounting methods to obtain the data required for evaluation. Some authorities[3] describe such methods as 'objective'.

Chapter 8 looks at methods which put more emphasis on the process of obtaining agreement on objectives through a process of exploration and mutual learning. Numbers are less important than a thorough understanding of the issues – the opportunities provided by the projected changes as well as the threats of failure or the possible disadvantages which the change may bring to some stakeholders. Such methods are labelled by the same authorities as 'subjective' methods.

The methods and approaches

A brief description of some of the more commonly used or interesting approaches is provided below.

Cost/revenue analysis

The most basic and hence widely used method is cost/revenue analysis.[4] The method uses conventional cost and management accounting procedures, including the types of measurement and valuation methods used in cost accounting. The costs of developing, implementing and operating the system are estimated and compared with the value of the benefits it is anticipated the system will generate. The method is used where the benefits can be directly attributed to the change of system and are realized in the form of cost savings, cost displacement, or, where this can be directly related to the change, additional revenue generated.

The method incorporates the following steps:

1 Estimate the cost of developing and implementing the system. The cost of managing the project must be included in the estimate. Most approaches use a model of the system's life-cycle for this purpose. Some tools for estimating project costs are now available. They include parametric estimation techniques based on a statistical analysis of many previous projects. The best known of these is the COCOMO method developed by Barry Boehm. Alternative methods are based on a measure of the complexity of the project. Best known of these is the function point analysis of Albrecht. Modern case tools often incorporate cost estimation models in their tool kit.

   In practice many evaluators rely on their experience from earlier projects and take the complexity of the project and the experience of the project staff into account when arriving at a cost estimate.

   Despite considerable experience in making cost estimates of information projects and the availability of estimating tools, it is still very difficult to produce reliable estimates, and variances of 100% still occur.
2 Estimate the expected life of the system – the time until the system has to be replaced because of technological obsolescence or because it can no longer be adjusted to meet the needs of the organization. In practice estimating the life of the system is hazardous. Many evaluations use a notional life expectancy of five or seven years to fit into the norm for investment projects in the organization.
3 Estimate the cost of operating the system once it has been implemented. The costs of operating the system must include the cost of maintaining the system. Work measurement and O&M techniques are perfectly adequate for estimating the straightforward operating

costs, but they are of little help in assessing likely maintenance costs. Some of the estimating tools referred to above also attempt to estimate maintenance costs. In practice these vary with the age of the system, and the cost of keeping the system in line with other developments in the organization rises sharply as the system ages.

The reliability of the estimate of the lifetime costs of the system depends on how good the estimate of the expected life of the system is.

4 Estimate the value of the benefits the system should generate. The method is most often used where the benefits can be directly attributed to the change in system and are realized in the form of savings or displaced costs. Staff savings are often calculated using work measurement and O&M techniques. Other methods of estimation include standard statistical or OR methods, such as those used, for example, for estimating the reduction in inventory resulting from a changed inventory control system.

Where the benefits are less tangible, e.g. the benefits from the reduction in stockouts in an inventory control system, assumptions may be made on the net extra sales generated by the reduction and the extra profit realized from the extra sales. Some managements would not permit such estimates to be used, but rely only on benefits which do not require assumptions of this kind.

5 Tabulate the costs and savings per time period over the expected life of the system and compare them.

The data collected and tabulated can subsequently be used to perform investment analysis using ROI-type techniques, described in the next section.

A variation of the method, SESAME,[5] has been proposed by IBM. In this method the cost–benefit from a project is derived by computing what the cost would have been if the same functionality as the proposed system had been delivered by non-computer-based methods. The net benefit is the computed cost minus the costs of the new system. Net benefits computed by the method result in very high returns on the capital employed and very short payback periods. A more relevant method might be to compare the costs and functionality of the proposed system with the costs and functionality of the 'second best' system. Such a comparison would show the extra value added of going from the second best system to the proposed system.

Return on investment (ROI) appraisal[6]

All ROI methods are based on the proposition that an investment now must yield a positive return over a period of time and most add that money held now has more value than the same amount received at some future date. Hence there is a discount rate which expresses the notion that the longer a return is deferred the lower is its current value. Many managements define in advance the return expected from any investment and the time over which the return must be achieved. ROI methods permit a management to compare the returns from a range of investment opportunities and select the ones which provide the best returns. The method also permits management to assess the degree of success of existing projects meeting the target (or benchmark) ROI criteria. ROI is applied to many types of capital expenditure decisions, and in many organizations the method is used as the standard way of deciding which capital expenditure projects are given the green light and which are halted.

ROI approaches are supported by a number of formal investment appraisal techniques. The best known are those which are based on evaluating the current value of estimated future cash flows on the assumption that future benefits are subject to a chosen discount factor. Two widely used methods are the discounted cash flow (DCF) method and the net present value (NPV) method. DCF and NPV calculations base their discount rate on an interest rate regarded as appropriate by the financial management of the organization. Many organizations which use the methods establish a rate of return which all projects must exceed if they are to be adopted. Such a rate is often known as the *hurdle* rate.

A simpler method which does not require an assumption of interest rates, which is used quite frequently, simply requires a project to pay back its investment over a prescribed period. The calculation for *payback period* methods are simpler and more easily understood by some stakeholders, but the method leaves out of account the notion that money has an opportunity cost.

ROI methods require the estimation of cash flow. Hence they tend to be based on data which satisfy accounting criteria and which are legitimized by appearing in financial statements. Ideally they are data which can be traced through the organization's accounting system. Intangibles cannot be dealt with in this way, and thus the method favours directly attributable benefits, often, but not necessarily, in the form of cost savings. Other methods, e.g. cost revenue analysis, can be used to provide the data for the various ROI techniques.

ROI methods tend to be used by organizations with tight financial disciplines. The techniques are formal, and the calculations are usually carried out by financial or accounting staff on the basis of inputs from the project staff. Although the DCF and NPV methods appear to cope with the problem of risk by the choice of discount rate, in practice the methods are not good at dealing with projects which have large elements of uncertainty in their projections.

ROI methods work best:

- when the application under review is expected to deliver direct savings or directly attributable revenue benefits
- when the estimates can be supported by reliable calculations or demonstrations, i.e. when there is low uncertainty regarding the outcomes
- where there are many competing projects demanding investment resources and there is a need to be able to compare the potential outcomes of the different projects on a standard financial basis.

Conversely the method is least good:

- where benefits cannot be precisely estimated in cash flow terms
- where there is considerable uncertainty about the value of the estimates
- where the timescales of projects differ markedly
- where intangible benefits are given a zero value because they cannot easily be expressed in cash flow terms. As Robert Kaplan states:[7]

> Although intangible benefits may be difficult to quantify, there is no reason to value them at zero in a capital expenditure analysis. Zero is, after all, no less arbitrary than any other analysis. Conservative accountants who assign zero values to many intangible benefits prefer being precisely wrong to being vaguely right. Managers need not follow their example.

Indeed, some of the IT projects which are exemplars of achieved competitive advantage would not have satisfied an evaluation procedure based on prevailing ROI criteria.

Cost–benefit analysis

A more sophisticated version of cost/revenue analysis is cost–benefit analysis.[8] Cost–benefit analysis is a method which tries to overcome the problem of valuing intangibles by imputing a money value for each element contributing to the costs and benefits of an IT project. The approach originated as an attempt to deal with two problems:

1 The problem of identifying the value of benefits (or costs) which do not directly accrue to the investor in the project, the so-called 'external economies', which add value or costs to the project. A good example of external costs is the extra pollution cost from putting an additional car on the road, paid for by society, and not the motorist. A good example of external benefits is the savings in road and building maintenance stemming from the introduction of a bypass to a town. Although external economies may occur in business projects,

the value added externally is not usually of interest to the investor. However, many public sector projects are expected to deliver benefits to the community at large and these must be considered when decisions about public sector investments are made.

2 Some elements regarded as a benefit or cost have no obvious market value or price – the classic example is the value that should be attached to a system which could result in the saving of one extra life. Projects involving decisions of that kind regularly occur in relation to information systems projects in the field of medical informatics. The general problem of attaching values to intangibles is one that is met in nearly all information systems projects.

The method:

- attempts to find some surrogate measure for intangible cost or benefit which can be expressed in money terms. Thus if one of the objectives of introducing a system is to increase the job satisfaction of office workers, the benefit may be expressed in terms of the saving in recruitment and training costs stemming from a hoped-for reduction in office staff turnover.

  A good example of the use of the method was the study (the Roskill Report) on the siting of London's third airport. Money values were assigned to the cost of noise pollution in the vicinity of a new airport by some prediction of the impact of noise pollution on property values. The cost of noise pollution was deemed to be the difference between the aggregate property value before the construction of the airport and the aggregate value estimated once the airport had been constructed. Although the measure only poorly reflects residents' perception of the 'real' cost of noise pollution, it provides at least a standard which could be used for all potential airport sites.[9]
- estimates cash flows on the basis of the notional valuations and these provide the data for a subsequent ROI appraisal.
- requires expert analysts to carry out the study. The study of a situation with many possible intangible costs and benefits can take a long time and involve considerable controversy and discussion.

The method is of particular value:

- where many of the costs and benefits are intangible.
- where there is broad agreement on the measures used to attach a value to the intangibles.

Conversely the method falls down:

- where there are widely different views on the intrinsic value of the intangibles and disagreement on the appropriate form of surrogate money value. The point is highlighted by the case of a well-known type of automobile. The manufacturing company decided not to alter the design of the car – a car which had a design weakness resulting in passenger death or injury with certain types of accident – because cost–benefit analysis suggested that the cost of redesign exceeded the cost the company faced from liability claims from deaths or injuries. However, the car-buying public put a different value on the deaths and injuries and stopped buying that particular type of car.

- where there is considerable uncertainty about the realization of the intangible benefits.

Return on management (ROM)[10]

Return on management is based on the notion that the real value of management information systems is that they enhance management productivity. The method therefore sets out to establish the increase in management productivity, measured as value added by management which can result from the introduction of new systems. The method is intended to supplant ROI as an investment appraisal technique for IT systems. It relies on obtaining estimates of cash flows from standard evaluation methods and financial statements and assigning the value added from each systems feature to a part of the value chain. Any value left over is the value imputed to management. In other words the economic value of management is the residue left after everyone else has been paid. The values computed are money values derived from the standard accounting and non-financial data held by an organization.

At the strategy formulation stage changes in ROM must be based on an estimate of revenue after the change is implemented and estimates of changes to resource costs and contributions. The difficulty of making such estimates suggests that the ROM method of evaluation is better suited to *ex post* evaluation of information systems projects. However, given a large data base of such *ex post* computations – Strassmann has based his findings on the PIMMS data base – it is possible to classify projects in order to associate types of application with ROM and thus help to define which type of application appears to have the best chance of achieving a high ROM.

In practice one of the most significant findings of Paul Strassmann was that an increase in the value added by management was associated with a high value of ROM before the changes were implemented. Conversely, low starting values of ROM tended to be associated with reductions in the value added by management following the introduction of new technology. If ROM measures management capability the results suggest that one of the most important critical success factors in the introduction of IT is management understanding and capability, both in a general sense of the business process and in the particular sense of appreciating the opportunities which IT can provide and knowing how to take advantage of them.

The advantage of the method is that it concentrates attention on the management process. The disadvantage is that the residue assigned as the value added by management cannot be directly attributed to the management process. The observed change in the value added by management may be the consequence of any number of other factors. For example, short-term fluctuations in revenue not matched by equivalent changes in resources employed may have a dominant impact on the residue defined as the value added by management.

Although the method requires data gathering, as most of the data come from established sources, the cost of computing ROM is not great. It may well be best used as a supplement to some of the more orthodox methods, in particular for *ex post* evaluations.

ROM provides interesting insights, but is not, because of the absence of any kind of causal rationale, in practice a serious contender as an evaluation technique.

Boundary values or spending ratios[11]

Boundary values or spending ratios are intended to provide a crude but simple view of how an enterprise or one division within an enterprise compares to its peer enterprises (or peer divisions) in the same industrial sector. They are based on ratios of total expenditure against known aggregate values. Typical ratios include total IT expenditure against

- the value of sales
- total labour costs
- total operating expenses
- total value of assets
- total value of deposits (for banks).

Such ratios may also be used to compare the use of IT within the strategic business units of one enterprise. Any strategic business unit whose expenditure ratio departs significantly from the average for the enterprise has to explain and account for the difference. Thus a higher IT cost to revenue ratio might be justified if it is matched by a higher benefit to cost ratio.

Often the ratios are used to check the level of use of IT in one enterprise as against the level of use in the industry sector to which the enterprise belongs. The value of the method is that a management can judge its position relative to its competitors very quickly, and can launch further investigations if it finds that it has an abnormal spending pattern.

The ratios are used in two ways:

1 They can be used as a rough guide on what level of IT expenditure to aim for in the enterprise. If the average expenditure ratio for the industry sector is much higher it suggests that the enterprise in question is not making sufficient use of IT. At the very least an investigation of what opportunities the enterprise is missing out on should be instigated. If the ratio is significantly higher than the industry average it suggests that further investment increases should be reviewed with extra care, and that current expenditure should be carefully examined to check what might be cut out. Of course, as American Airlines demonstrated in the early 1980s, a higher ratio can be associated with a significantly higher benefit. In that case the higher expenditure ratio reflected the competitive advantage American Airlines obtained from the introduction of the SABRE system of airline reservations for travel agents.
2 They can be used to check on the efficiency of the enterprise's IT group. A higher than average ratio suggests the group is using IT resources less efficiently than the industry as a whole. A low ratio could suggest efficient use, in particular if the enterprise is seen to be a successful user of information systems.

The main advantage of boundary value methods is that they provide a relatively cheap and easily understood way of alerting management that further analysis is necessary. The disadvantage of the methods is that the comparisons based on spending ratios provide no explanatory information and do not provide any comparisons of the effectiveness of the systems employed by the peer group. Further industry averages can hide considerable variations in individual results. Hence the value of these averages as a guide to policy making must be treated with caution. At best they can suggest the need for a much more thoroughgoing investigation.

A more convincing guide to policy making or even as a check that the enterprise is on the right track with regard to the level of use of IT would be a comparison with the ratios of the enterprise's most competitive rival.

Information economics[12]

Information economics was developed by Parker and Benson to cope with some of the difficulties people had described in attempting to evaluate IT projects. As such it seeks to be the one and only method capable of coping with the IT evaluation jungle. In practice the method is a variant of cost–benefit analysis, tailored to cope with the particular intangibles and uncertainties found in information systems projects. It retains ROI calculations for those benefits and costs which can be directly ascertained through a conventional cost–benefit process, but puts forward for the decision process a more complex report based on a ranking and scoring technique of intangibles and risks. The ROI outcome is itself given a score, enabling the executives to provide a relative evaluation of tangibles as against intangibles. It seeks, in other words, to identify, measure or rank the economic impact of all the changes on organizational performance thought to be relevant brought about by the introduction of new systems.

Normal cost–benefit analysis is extended by three processes. The first is called *value linking*. The method looks for the consequential impact of a primary change spreading through a range of functional departments. For example, the introduction of JIT has a primary impact on the control of inventory. But it will reduce the number of invoices which have to be dealt with by the purchase function, and reduce account entries by the accounts department. If the JIT system also increases the risks of halting the line because of a delivery delay that impact can also be brought into the equation.

The second process is called by the authors *value acceleration*. Value acceleration attempts to define the value of future systems which are dependent on the introduction of the system in question. Thus the primary impact of an inventory control system may be enhanced if that system is also seen to be the platform on which a later EDI system can be built. The introduction of the inventory control system may bring forward the time at which a full EDI system could be introduced, thus accelerating the future value. The question asked is: will a separate, future system realize benefits sooner if the current proposal is accepted?

The third process is called *job enrichment*. The process provides an evaluation of the additional value to the organization of the enhanced skills and understanding which its staff may gain from the use of IT. The case of the defence contractor described in Chapter 5 provides a first-class example of the value of job enrichment. The DTP system acquired by the company enabled engineers to produce their own copy. It increased job satisfaction, cut costs, improved product quality, and enabled the company to compete in areas previously thought to be too difficult for them.

In a sense, information economics links the quantification and comparison emphasis of the methods described in this chapter with the more exploratory methods defined in Chapter 8. The method is comprehensive in its treatment of benefits and risks. It applies both innovation and investment evaluation when the financial issues change from measuring to evaluation of and choosing amongst new, untried and unproven alternatives. On the cost side it recognizes strategic uncertainty, organizational risk, definitional uncertainty and technological uncertainty as cost elements which have to be included in the analysis.

The advantage of the method is that it provides capabilities for dealing with many of the identified problems. It requires considerable expertise to use and can be expensive in use in that it requires in-depth analysis of many possibilities such as tracing the possible consequential impact of a change. The method is probably not practical for use in classes of systems (see Chapter 9) where the problem of evaluation hinges on finding the best system to perform a closely defined task. For the more simple transaction-processing system with direct, tangible benefits the method may prove too complex. However, some of the useful notions, such as value linking and job enrichment, introduced in information economics can be used without employing the full rigour of the method.

Notes and references

1 The COCOMO method as developed by Barry Boehm is based on a statistical analysis of over 600 large projects. Boehm was able to express the estimated costs of a software construction process by a series of equations linking relevant variables, such as likely programme size, to use of resources. The function point method was developed by Albrecht and is based on a measure of the object system's complexity expressed in the form of the system's functions.

2 Variance analysis is used by Enid Mumford in her ETHICS methodology. Its use in the identification of actual or potential problems (variance) is described in: Mumford, E. (1983) *Designing Human Systems: The ETHICS Method*, Manchester Business School.

3 Powell, P. (1992) Information technology evaluation: is it different? *Journal of the Operational Research Society*, **43**, No. 1. Powell's classification differs from ours in that some of the methods which he defines as objective, we regard as belonging to the subjective category.

4 Cost/revenue analysis is explained in most cost accounting textbooks. Useful books are: Shillinglaw, G. (1982) *Managerial Cost Accounting*, Irwin, Homewood; Horngren, C. T. and Sundem, G. I. (1987) *Introduction to Management Accounting*, 3rd edn, Prentice Hall, Hemel Hempstead.

5 SESAME is described in: Lincoln, T. (1986) Do computer systems really pay off? *Information and Management*, **11**, No. 1, 25–34.

6 Almost any of a large number of textbooks on financial management provide an introduction to ROI methods. A good introduction is provided in: Radcliffe, R. C. (1982) *Investment: Concepts, Analysis, Strategy*, Scott, Foreman and Co, Glenview, Illinois.

7 Kaplan, R. (1986) Must CIM be justified by faith alone, *Harvard Business Review*, **64**, No. 2, 87–95.

8 The seminal paper on the use of cost–benefit techniques for information systems is: Emery, J. (1973) Cost benefit analysis of information systems, *SMIS Workshop*, No. 1. A good review of the methods can be found in: King, J. L. and Schrems, E. L. (1978) Cost–benefit analysis in information systems development and operation, *Computing Surveys*, March, 19–34.

9 A good discussion of some of the shortcomings of cost–benefit analysis used as in the Roskill Report can be found in: Self, P. (1970) Nonsense on stilts: the futilities of Roskill, *New Society*, July, 8–11; Stern, G. T. A. (1976) SOSOping or sophistical obfuscation of self-interest and prejudice, *Operational Research Quarterly*, **27**, No. 4(ii), 915–929. A defence of cost–benefit methods is provided by: Abrahams, S. B., Flowerdew, A. D. J. and Smith, J. U. M. (1978) Correspondence on SOSOPing of sophistical obfuscation of self-interest and prejudice, *Journal of the Operational Research Society*, **29**, No. 2, 173–178.

10 The best rationale for the method is provided in: Strassmann, P. (1985) *Information Payoff: The Transformation of Work in the Electronic Age*, The Free Press, New York. The book also provides one of the most important studies of the impact of IT on more than 300 North American corporations.

11 A study of ratios within industry sectors was carried out by Rod Martin: Martin, R. (1989) *The Utilisation and Efficiency of IS: A Comparative Analysis*, Oxford Institute of Information Management, Templeton College, Oxford. Paul Strassmann[10] has made extensive use of spending ratios in his study of North American corporations. He plots a variety of spending ratios for individual companies within industry sectors against measures of productivity for the same companies.

12 Information economics is described by its developers in articles and books. The fullest explanation of the method is provided in: Parker, M. M. and Benson, R. J. (1987) *Information Economics*, Prentice Hall, Englewood Cliffs, New Jersey. A shorter version, providing the main flavour of the method, is provided as: Parker, M. M. and Benson, R. J. (1987) Information economics: an introduction, *Datamation*, December, 89–96.

8 Evaluation methods: exploratory and experimental techniques

Introduction

In this chapter we describe a number of techniques which emphasize the *process* by which the relevant criteria for decision-making and review are arrived at. Most of the techniques described involve a wide range of individuals – the 'stakeholders' who are involved in the project as sponsors, designers, implementers, users and operators, as well as those who are affected by the system under review in a more indirect way. Some methods stress the need for involving the stakeholders in group meetings. All the methods provide a valuable opportunity for stakeholders to enhance their common understanding of the issues, and perhaps to gain new skills and competencies. Above all many of these methods provide an opportunity for individual and organizational learning, thus helping the organization to operate more effectively; they enrich the process layer described in Chapter 6.

The methods

Multi-objective, multi-criteria methods[1]

Multi-objective, multi-criteria (MOMC) methods are often regarded as alternatives to cost–benefit analysis. They start from the recognition that there are measures of worth other than money values. Hence the methods attempt to define a general measure of 'utility' where utility is defined as the satisfaction of an individual's revealed preferences. Utility is a measure of satisfaction. Aggregate utility is the sum of individual utility. Where there are many stakeholders the best system is that which is expected to deliver the highest aggregate utility – that which provides the highest overall measure of satisfied preferences.

The approach is grounded in the view that peoples' behaviour is determined to an extent by their feeling that their preferences are recognized. They can, and do, appraise the relative usefulness of different desired outcomes in terms of their preferences – and they explicitly or tacitly rank goals by applying a preference weight to each goal. Preferences may result from the stakeholders' evaluation of what is good for the organization mixed up with a desire for more personal benefits. Desired outcomes can be represented in a number of forms and with varying degrees of precision.

The approach recognizes:

(a) that different stakeholders may have different views or judgements on the value of some output from the proposed system, e.g. the value added by having information about a production variance on the day the variance occurred rather than two days later.
(b) that many users find it easier to express their preferences in relative terms rather than in money values. Thus the works manager may express a strong preference for having the variance report at least one day earlier than at present but only a weak preference for having it on the day the variance occurs. Users can attach relative weights to desirable outcomes rather than money values.

   Similarly the user can evaluate a preference by means of relative weights for different possible outputs from the system. Thus an accountant may put a high relative value on a system which can save costs directly as against the objective of providing the works manager with earlier production variance reports.

Even a direct measure – say the contribution to net profits of a reduction in headcount – may have different value for different people. It may be regarded by the financial director as of equivalent value to an equal contribution to net profits from an increase in sales delivered by an alternative system. The chief executive, however, may see the reduction in headcount as providing more value because it provides a reduction of the cost base which is important for maintaining the competitive position of the company. On the other hand the personnel director may prefer the new sales system because he fears the reduction in headcount will stir up discontent and alienate the workforce.

The approach permits an exploration of these different viewpoints and allows, for example, the stakeholders to express in an explicit form the value of reducing the cost base as against the value of avoiding an alienated workforce. Issues are aired within the content of an 'evaluation party'.[2] Potential conflict is exposed at the exploratory stage in a project's life-cycle rather than having it emerge after the system has been implemented. Exposing differences provides the first step towards attempting to achieve a consensus.

The advantages of the method include the following:

• The possibility of exploring the value of a set of system proposals in terms of relative preferences for different system features.

- Achieving consensus on the most desired system attributes by means of a thorough exploration of alternatives and preferences.
- Arriving at a decision by evaluating preferences and choosing the system which provides the highest satisfaction in terms of weighted preferences.

The disadvantages of the method include the following:

- The method does not provide any data for an ROI calculation. That means that it is difficult to compare an investment justified by the use of a standard cost–benefit approach with one justified by using the MOMC method. The method does not show the return on a proposal in terms which will satisfy an accountant or which give results in terms of the bottom line.
- The method involves a great deal of discussion and can be costly.

MOMC is probably best applied to complex projects which attempt to meet the needs of many different users and where the benefits are intangible. It can be supported by a number of computer-based decision support systems.[3] A number of organizations have used the method in conjunction with decision conferencing, which permits a group of people to explore and model their preferences. The use of sensitivity analysis can demonstrate that in many cases conflict on objectives and values does not have any effect on the outcome of the decision process.

Value analysis[4]

Value analysis is another way of attempting to establish a value for the outputs of the system. The method emphasizes benefits rather than costs and is used primarily for evaluating concepts such as 'better information'. It begins with the observation that most successful innovations are based on enhancing value added rather than on saving costs. To get at value the intangibles must be assessed. Value analysis suggests that there are two types of intangibles:

1 The decision maker's ability to make 'better' decisions with the new system in place.
2 The value added to the organization if decisions are better.

The method uses a variety of techniques to establish value. They are used in an iterative, exploratory manner. One element of this is to use a Delphi approach. This involves asking 'experts' – perhaps the managers for whom the system is being designed – to speculate on their use of the proposed system and to suggest the value of any improved performance on their own part. The views of a number of managers may vary quite widely. However, the Delphi approach confronts all of the managers with the speculations of their fellow managers. A new round of consultation with the same experts is likely to show modified viewpoints. After a number of iterations a consensus tends to emerge which is then regarded as the most likely outcome.

A further step is to build a prototype of the system in order to gain more experience of the way stakeholders might use the system. If the cost of building the prototype is regarded as too high the new system may be simulated and used in a game-playing mode or with role-playing by a range of potential users. Each 'experiment', prototype, management game, or simulation provides further clues on the likely value that the system may contribute to the organization. It is worth noting that the more the proposed system differs from the system it is replacing, the greater the uncertainty of the impact of the system and the more important it is to iterate through the stages of discovery.

Where the proposed system is expected to deliver a variety of benefits – for example, the system is expected to help managers to make better purchasing decisions and to improve the relations between the buying company and the supplier – the value analysis groups the benefits into homogeneous groups using the statistical technique of cluster analysis. Having summarized the benefits in their separate groups a value has to be determined for the group as a whole. Since the benefits are expressed in a variety of forms – some linguistic, some numeric – a common measure must be found. Like MOMC, value analysis permits the calculation of utilities by attaching utility scores to each group.

The main advantages of the method are:

- Establishing agreed values for outputs which would normally be classed as intangible.
- Providing decision makers with some kind of assurance that the benefits can be realized by means of prototype demonstrations or Delphi processes. It is a method of reducing uncertainty.
- Values can be expressed in money terms and hence can enter into an ROI appraisal; alternatively the method accepts systems of valuation based on utility measures.

The disadvantages of the method are:

- Establishing values can be a lengthy and costly exercise.
- Concern about the accuracy of procedures such as the Delphi method.

However, whichever method is chosen, it is difficult to be accurate where benefits are dependent on the behaviour of users in relation to new or different informational outputs.

Critical success factors

One of the most popular methods for exploring the potential value of information systems is based on Rockart's notion of critical success factors.[5] The method invites the analyst to explore with executives those factors which are in their opinion critical to the success of the business, in particular those that are important for the functions or activities for which the executives are responsible. Issues can be ranked by the executives into levels of importance. By addressing critical issues the method gains the attention of the relevant executives right up to the level of the chief executive. The importance of the method is that it provides a focus on the issues which the respondents regard as important – the ones they will back if it comes to a choice of issues which have to be dealt with. The analyst can go on to examine the extent to which IT can be used to support the executive in dealing with the critical issues.

Experimental methods

The use of experimental methods is a recent development in the context of information systems project evaluation, though some of the methods have been used for evaluation in other situations. Until recently the precise impact of introducing new systems could only be estimated *ex ante* because the investment in developing a system to the stage of getting actual impacts was very high. Today a range of software development tools and simulation methods make it possible to develop a prototype or model of the new system rapidly and cheaply. This enables the designer to test and modify the system and its impacts experimentally before decisions on introducing a fully engineered version have to be taken. It permits the project champion to demonstrate a working model of the system to sceptical users or to senior management who need to see the system before they will underwrite it.

There are three main categories of experimental methods:

1 *Prototyping*[6] involves the rapid development of a prototype form of the system, typically using a fourth-generation language for the development. The prototype is tested and evaluated and, if necessary, modified and tested again. Prototyping is best used where the impact of the proposed system is highly uncertain. Often they are systems which are innovatory and where the use of the system is discretionary. The use of prototypes lends itself to discovering how users modify their behaviour when provided with, for example, a decision support system.
2 *Simulation*[7] probably has the longest history in information system evaluation. It involves formulating the projected system in the form

of a model, and using simulation as a basis for the experiment. Simulation can be very important for IT projects in that it allows sensitivity analysis which can help to resolve problems about the robustness of the proposed system in the face of uncertain assumptions.

3 *Game-playing* and *role-playing*[8] can be used to assess the outcome of a new way of doing certain tasks. Rather than get involved in the expense of building a prototype, a mail order company uncertain on how its clerical workforce or its middle management would respond to a proposed scheme to introduce office automation asked both management and clerks to role-play each others' jobs, first with existing systems, and then with the new office systems in mind. The outcome was a much clearer appreciation by management and staff of what the new system could accomplish and, equally important, what it would not be able to do. This made it possible to provide a much better assessment of the value of office automation to the mail order company.

Composite and *ad hoc* methods

The literature also described a number of what can best be called composite and *ad hoc* methods[9] which incorporate aspects of many of the methods outlined in Chapters 7 and 8. In practice many organizations combine parts of a number of methods and vary the methods to suit the situation. They often use short cuts or approaches they have developed themselves.

The *ad hoc* methods can be classified as:

• *Top-down strategic*: Senior management believes that IT is fundamental to the success of the organization and any evaluation is based on conviction rather than analysis.
• *Top-down by mandate*: Strategic business units often have little discretion in their investments in IT. Corporate headquarters (sometimes located abroad) lay down what is to be done, and a strategic business unit has little or no choice but to comply.
• *Incremental change*: The next step is determined by technological change or obsolescence. Evaluation is limited to determining when the next technical upgrade is to be introduced.
• *Competitive imperative*: The organization must follow in the footsteps of its competitors to survive – 'got to do'.
• *Pick and mix*: The advocates for a new or changed system pick from evaluation strategies those which they believe maximize their chance of a favourable decision.

Table 8.1 A summary of methods and techniques

Method	Level of detail required	Management process or method	Data characteristics	Features of method
Cost/revenue analysis	Very detailed	Accounting and costing staff	Cost accounting and work-study methods	Concentrates on cost savings and cost displacement
Return on investment (ROI)	High	Calculation by professionals; enumerates tangible costs and benefits and aggregates these as cash flows	Tangible; direct; objective	*Ex ante* and *ex post*. Takes account of future uncertainty. Middle to high cost
Cost–benefit analysis	High	Bottom up; carried out by experts; provides money values for decision makers by incorporating surrogate measures	Enumerates cost and benefit elements and expresses them in a standard money value form; pseudo-objective	*Ex ante* or *ex post*. Selects cost-effective solutions; copes with 'external' and 'soft' costs and benefits; numbers are more important than process; provides input into return on investment calculations. High cost
Return on management (ROM)	Low	Calculation by professionals; manipulates accounting figures to produce a residue – value added by management	Accounting totals, e.g. total revenue, total labour cost	*Ex post*. No cause and effect relations can be postulated; applies a formula. Cheap
Boundary values and spending ratios	Low; aggregate	Top-down. Involves senior stakeholders; calculation by professionals	Ratios of aggregated numbers, e.g. IT spend per employee	*Ex ante* or *ex post*. Good for comparisons with competitors, or others in same industry sector. Cheap

Method	Level/detail	Process	Evaluation	Comments
IE, information economics	Can be very detailed	Involves many stakeholders. Requires detailed analysis	Permits ranking and rating of objectives, both tangible and intangible	Deals comprehensively with all options. Hence rather complex
MOMC, multi-objective, multi-criteria	Any level	Top-down; explores perceptions; consensus seeking; involves all stakeholders; computes best choice, helped by expert facilitator	Stakeholders revealed preferences; uses subjective evaluations of intangibles	*Ex ante*. Good for extracting softer requirements; process is more important than numbers; helps select (a) preferred set of design goals, (b) best design alternative. High cost
Value analysis	Any level; generally detailed	Iterative. Involves senior to middle management; relevant variables and their values are identified using a Delphi method	Indirect; includes subjective evaluations of intangibles; uses utility scores	*Ex ante*. Iterative. Incremental; concentrates more on value added than on costs saved; process is more important than numbers. High cost
Critical success factors	Short list of factors	Senior management define CSFs	Interview or self-expression. Quick but takes up senior management time	*Ex ante*. Highly selective
Experimental methods	Can vary from detailed to abstract	Management scientists working with stakeholders	Exploratory. Reduces uncertainty	*Ex ante*

The prevalence of *ad hoc* methods, not to mention 'got-to-do' and 'act-of-faith' methods, reminds us that in many organizations the formal evaluation process is part of a game played between those who have an interest in getting approval for a pet IT project and the decision makers. The advocates of the project collect the information they think is needed to gain approval of the project. Often the information is contrived, but difficult to attack because it is underpinned by arguments based on strategic necessity, or what competitors are supposed to be up to. On the other hand, resistant decision makers will ask for more hard data, and will expect precise quantification of benefits, even where the case for the change is made on the basis of second-order effects. Who wins the game depends on political rather than business factors.

Table 8.1 summarizes the methods and techniques described in Chapters 7 and 8.

Notes and references

1 Much has been written about multi-criteria, multi-objective decision-making in the field of the management sciences. A good, but somewhat mathematical, exposition is: Kenny, R. L. and Raiffa, H. (1976) *Decisions with Multiple Objectives: Preferences and Value Tradeoffs*, John Wiley and Sons, New York. With regard to information systems evaluation, the method is explained in a number of papers. We have selected the following: Land, F. F. (1976) Evaluation of systems goals in determining a design strategy for a computer based information system, *Computer Journal,* **19**, No. 4, 290–294; Vaid-Raizda, V. K. (1983) Incorporation of intangibles in computer selection decisions, *Journal of Systems Management,* **34**, No. 11, 30–46; Chandler, J. S. (1982) A multiple criteria approach for evaluating information systems, *MIS Quarterly,* **6**, No. 1, 61–74.

2 A. J. Gregory and M. C. Jackson introduce the term 'evaluation party' in their description of an evaluation process in which the varying characteristics of those involved generate different evaluation contexts. See; Gregory, A. J. and Jackson, M. C. (1992) Evaluation methodologies: a system for use, *Journal of the Operational Research Society,* **43**, No. 1, 19–28.

3 Multi-objective, multi-criteria methods are quite complex and require a considerable amount of calculation. Hence a number of support tools have been developed. L. Phillips, one of the pioneers of using the method within a decision conferencing context, has written about the method and provided a number of useful case studies.

4 Value analysis is well described in a number of papers. These include: Melone, N. P. and Wharton, T. J. (1984) Strategies for MIS project selection, *Journal of Systems Management,* **32**, No. 2, 26–37; Money, A., Tromp, D. and Wegner, T. (1988) The quantification of decision support benefits within the context of value analysis, *MIS Quarterly,* **12**, No. 2, 223–236; Rivard, E. and Kaiser, K. (1989) The benefits of quality IS, *Datamation*, January, 53–58.

5 Jack Rockart introduced his method in 1979: Rockart, J. (1979) Chief executives define their own information needs, *Harvard Business Review,* **57**, No. 2, 81–93. Since then the notion that we can identify critical success factors has become popular and widely used. It is probably the best known and widest used purely exploratory technique.

6 Prototyping is widely discussed in the technical literature. However, the main focus of most of the literature is not on evaluation. Useful material can be found in: Alavi, M. (1984) An assessment of the prototyping approach to information systems development, *Communications of the ACM*, **27**, No. 6, 556–563; Earl, M. (1978) Prototype systems for accounting, information and control, *Accounting, Organisation and Control*, **3**, No. 2, 161–170.

7 Much of the literature on simulation comes from the domain of management science and OR and has little to say on simulation used for evaluation. An interesting paper on the use of simulation for risk assessment is: Hertz, D. B. (1990) Risk analysis in capital investment, in *Strategic Planning: Models and Analytical Techniques* (ed. G. R. Dyson), John Wiley and Sons, Chichester, pp. 121–138. Attention was first drawn to the potentiality of using simulation for evaluation in: Kleijnen, J. P. C. (1979) Evaluation of management information systems, *Omega*, **7**, No. 6, 539–543.

8 The use of role playing is discussed with examples in: Hirschheim, R. A. (1985) *Office Automation: A Social and Organisational Perspective*, Wiley Series in Information Systems, Chichester. A further useful paper is: Etzerodt, P. and Madsen, K. H. (1988) Information assessment as a learning process, in *Information Assessment: Issues and Challenges* (eds N. Bjorn-Andersen and G. Davis), North Holland, Amsterdam, pp. 333–347.

9 A good example of the use of composite methods is provided in: Schaefer, G. (1988) *Functional Analysis of Office Requirements: A Multi-perspective Approach*, Chapters 5 and 11, Wiley Series in Information Systems, Chichester. Further useful material comes from: Earl, M. (1989) *Management Strategies for Information Management*, Chapter 8, Prentice Hall, Englewood Cliffs, New Jersey.

Part Four

Part Four (Chapters 9–12) first turns the spotlight away from the evaluation methods which were the subject of Part Three and turns it onto the information system applications themselves. It then goes on to demonstrate a new approach to classifying information systems and to helping evaluators choose an appropriate mix of evaluation approaches and tools.

- **Chapter 9** classifies the characteristics of information systems applications and projects in a way which helps to identify suitable evaluation methods.
- **Chapter 10** identifies the factors which are most relevant to the choice of evaluation method.
- **Chapter 11** presents a new approach whose objective is to enable the evaluator to match the investment situation with an appropriate evaluation method.
- **Chapter 12** sets out our concluding thoughts.

9 Different types of project

Every organization is subject to a variety of forces which provide the triggers for change. Pressure for change may come from many sources – some originating inside the organization and some from the organization's environment. The reactive organization responds to the forces for change. The proactive organization may generate its own dynamic. IT is used in many ways as a response to the triggers and to achieve a wide range of different objectives. The different types of applications and the wide range of objectives suggest that we may need a wide range of evaluation methods, some suitable for evaluating one type of application and some more suitable for other types. Indeed, type of application and type of objective prove to be among the most influential factors in the choice of evaluation method. Classifying the uses of information systems may therefore be of help in selecting suitable evaluation methods.

Some authorities have classified applications according to a stages of growth model.[1] The underlying reasoning behind the stages of growth model is that there is a deterministic process which leads organizations along a predetermined path from simple cost-saving applications to more complex value added application projects and further to applications based on end-user computing. With hindsight one can indeed detect an apparent pattern of application types. However, the process is anything but deterministic and if there is a causal factor it is more tied to the availability of different types of technology. Advanced organizations today still choose to develop cost-saving applications. More technological options provide a wider range of possibilities than was available to planners 30 years ago. Nevertheless, a recent study found that nearly 70% of applications are still based on cost savings.[2]

We have chosen to present an alternative model.[3] The model postulates a kind of ladder. Each rung of the ladder represents a type of change and hence a type of application. The applications typical for each higher rung represent increasing potential benefits, but also increasing uncertainty on outcomes, increasing risk of failure and increasing difficulty of communicating the 'case' for change to relevant stakeholders. The focus of evaluation and the appropriate evaluation techniques are different for each rung of the ladder. Whereas precise quantification of costs and benefits are possible near the bottom of the ladder, the higher rungs rely more on experimental and judgemental processes. Risk assessment becomes an important component of evaluation near the top of the ladder. At the top of the ladder decisions require not merely the consent of the top management team but also their continuous involvement. They represent some of the most difficult activities faced by senior management.

Figure 9.1 illustrates the model. Each step of the ladder is explained in more detail below.

Rung 8	Business transformations
Rung 7	Strategic systems
Rung 6	Inter-organizational systems
Rung 5	Infrastructure
Rung 4	MIS and DSS systems
Rung 3	Direct value added
Rung 2	Automation
Rung 1	Mandatory changes

Figure 9.1 The project ladder

First rung: Mandatory changes

The bottom rung represents forced or mandatory changes. Decisions are confined to choosing from alternative designs. The task of evaluation is to provide technical assessments and costings of the alternative solutions. Three types of forced change affect information system decisions:

1 If the enterprise is under competitive pressure, perhaps because competitors have introduced new methods or improved customer service, it may be a *strategic necessity* to follow the competitor's lead.

Classic examples are banks adopting ATM (Automatic Teller Machine) technology, even though it is almost impossible to meet normal investment criteria for justifying the investment. Similarly it is strategically necessary for airlines and travel businesses to adopt IT-based reservation systems.

Once the situation has been recognized the role of evaluation is to find the 'best' system which will provide the required capability. This may result in the choice of a competitor's system and paying a royalty as happened when the success of the SABRE system, introduced by American Airlines (AA), drove other airlines to pay a royalty to AA in order to be allowed to use their system.

2 If the enterprise is forced to make certain technical changes or improvements it may be a *technological necessity* to adopt IT solutions.

Good examples of external pressure to make technical change come from the pressure to stop further deterioration of the environment. Car manufacturers have by law to provide new mechanisms for reducing the output of harmful emissions. These are in turn monitored and controlled by IT products.

Technological obsolescence is probably the most common reason for technological necessity. It arises when the cost of maintaining existing systems becomes prohibitive or new technology becomes available which clearly out-performs current technology.

Again the role of evaluation is to find the 'best' way of providing the new technology.

3 Certain changes in information systems are predetermined by regulation and legislation. They are cases of *regulatory* or *legal necessity*.

The changes required to meet the conditions of the privacy laws are mandatory and hence the role of evaluation is to assess the best method of implementing the legislation. Because the privacy laws are confined to information held on computer files the role of evaluation is extended to consider the alternative of returning to a manual filing system. Other examples are the rules which regulate a number of aspects of banking practice and procedures laid down by the European Community.

The most widely used methods of evaluation use classic cost accounting and work measurement techniques to evaluate the costs of the alternative solutions. However, problems stemming from the uncertainty of identifying the precise costs of innovatory technology make the process of choice hazardous and can result in choices based on false analysis.

Second rung: Automation

The next rung represents applications designed to replace existing methods in order to reduce costs. The process is one of automating existing routines. Historically they were often the first type of applications to use computers. Payroll is the standard example. In the 1950s and 1960s many organizations first used computers as replacements for punched card equipment to carry out exactly the same tasks but at a lower cost. Such applications tend to be concerned with transaction processing and generally handle large volumes of repetitive workloads. They may provide little in the way of new business approaches and they may not be directly part of the value chain and hence have little impact on the profitability of the business.

However, automation can have more important effects:

1 Reducing the cost base of a business may be an important strategic objective, and can provide competitive advantage. The most successful supermarket chain within a market niche may be the one which contrives to squeeze an extra fraction of a per cent of margin from its sales by means of its cost-saving information handling.
2 Increasing labour productivity, in particular the productivity of white collar labour, can dramatically increase the capacity of an enterprise, or indeed an industry, to manage growth. An example is the retail banking sector. The retail banks today handle vastly more transactions with a static or diminished workforce. At one time it was estimated that the workforce required to process the number of transactions now handled by the banking system would require virtually the whole of the country's white collar labour.

Many applications which now provide the essential, basic, factory-style, transaction processing of enterprises fall into this category.

Benefits are directly attributable to the replacement of the older methods and technology by the newer. The focus of evaluation is on efficiency and the most appropriate evaluation methods rely on classical work measurement and O&M techniques, supplemented by some OR methods (simulation and modelling). Whilst for many organizations these kinds of application provide the chief justification for the investment in IT-based systems, in many cases the actual outcome has been disappointing because the estimates of cost saving have neglected important, but often hidden, costs of co-ordination and troubleshooting.

Third rung: Direct value added

The third rung is represented by applications which not only reduce costs but add value directly, often by doing things which were not done before. They are intended to improve some aspects of business performance which had already been identified as 'valued'. The added value is directly attributable to the IT system. The additional value may be reflected in the increased margin the enterprise achieves on its turnover, or it may result in an increase in market share. Many value-adding applications automate existing processes but add some new features which add value. An interesting example of value added to payroll processing arose when a system produced a real-time print-out of earnings in a payment by output system. Productivity was enhanced because the workforce could see higher effort reflected in higher earnings. Many operational, transaction-processing types of application fall into this category. Typical of these applications is order processing, where enhanced facilities – e.g. providing small retailers with details of previous purchases – adds value both to the customer by improved customer service, and to the supplier.

Note, however, that the added value does not necessarily accrue to the enterprise. In a highly competitive situation, and where the technology is not protected by regulations or patents, the added value may benefit the consumer rather than the enterprise. Thus ATMs, which clearly add value to the banking system by making bank services available to clients 24 hours each day, seven days a week, have distributed that added value directly to the consumer, and not, on the whole, to the banks.

Adding value is an example of increasing effectiveness. The focus of evaluation is to assess what value is added and how that value might be distributed. But estimating the impact of the new capability often proves difficult. The banks did not foresee the impact that ATMs would have on their clients. The constant availability of the bank's services encouraged clients to go to the bank (the ATM) more frequently and, for example, to withdraw smaller amounts of cash several times per week instead of making one call per week as before. The outcome is that the bank has to process many more transactions without any change in the total value of transactions.

Classical cost accounting techniques and work measurement techniques do not provide useful estimates. Probably the best method of assessment is to use experimental techniques: for the banks field tests to gauge client response to the availability of the ATM service might have provided a better assessment of the actual impact of the innovation. However, competitive pressure may preclude the use of such techniques. Thomson Holidays owe at least some of their success in gaining competitive advantage with their TOPS package holiday booking system to the fact that they carefully pretested the system with selected travel agents before attempting a nation-wide launch of the system.

Fourth rung: Management information and decision support systems

The next rung represents applications which provide information for planning, control and decision-making. They are often directed at the higher levels of management.

In recent years emphasis has shifted from transaction processing – the automation of existing procedures – to using the technology to enhance the productivity of managers and other professional workers by providing them with quality – 'better' – information which enables them to control the business better and make better and more informed decisions. The word 'better' may mean more relevant information, more reliable information, more accurate information, more timely information, or information presented in a more easily used form. It can mean providing managers with possible scenarios of the future, or of evaluating alternative courses of action put forward by them. Such information is expected to improve the way a manager, or group of managers, carries out the tasks of planning, co-ordinating, controlling and general decision-making. A good example is the marketing information which supermarket management obtains through the introduction of EPOS systems.

The names given to applications in this category include management information systems, decision support systems, expert advisory systems, executive information systems and group decision support systems. The common features of applications representing the fourth rung is that they provide facilities which add value only if the users of the facilities have the capability (or opportunity) to take advantage of them. The fact that a manager has specified that 'better' information is a requirement is no guarantee that the better information will improve managerial productivity or added value. In many cases the use of such systems is discretionary, and merely discovering that managers choose to use the system is no guarantee of improved managerial outputs, though the fact that the systems are used in preference to alternative systems suggests that the users value the system.

The focus of evaluation becomes an assessment of the potential added value, framed perhaps by some kind of probability measure or best and worst case analysis. An alternative sometimes used is to ask the information users to assess the value of 'better' information and to back their judgement by 'paying' for the better information. Provided that payment is made from real resources, this is a useful device for, for example, profit centres. Further, it establishes a benchmark for subsequent evaluation and an incentive for the information user to achieve the potential benefit. However, viewed from a corporate perspective, the willingness to pay for the facility offers no guarantee that any extra value will accrue to the organization. The mechanism has simply transferred the responsibility for making a decision on the implementation of the new system from the provider to the payee.

In practice, evidence that fourth rung systems have appreciably enhanced managerial capability is difficult to obtain. One problem is finding appropriate data to evaluate outcomes. Experiments on, for example, the impact of decision support systems on the quality of decisions, carried out in controlled conditions, can never capture the richness and noisiness of the conditions under which managers have to work. A number of studies attempting to associate managerial productivity with investments in IT have found little evidence that managerial capability is enhanced by the use of IT. Perhaps the point to be made is that the most important aspect of managerial productivity is that managers should have a high competence in carrying out their substantive tasks – that the effective banker is not the one who has the best decision support system, but the one who has the highest skill in carrying out his banking tasks. The work of some researchers suggests that there is an association between high managerial capability and getting value from the use of fourth rung systems.

Fifth rung: Infrastructure

The fifth rung is represented by investments which provide a general capability, but may not be targeted at any specific application. They are intended to provide the foundation upon which subsequent value-adding applications can be built. Producing no *direct* benefits to the business, they may not figure prominently in the senior management's value system. A good example is the introduction of office automation into an enterprise. The expectation is that facilities like LANs, access to external facilities and data bases, Email, word-processing, graphics, DTP, the availability of spreadsheet capabilities, and local data base facilities, will enhance the productivity of the office. In some senses the facilities are used as part of the informal, undesigned systems which exist alongside more formal, designed systems in all organizations. Evidence of this trend comes from the use people make of Email. Many of the messages, in some cases as many as 50%, are personal messages; conversations between fellow workers.

Actual use of the facilities on offer will evolve through time, and actual use, enhanced efficiency and potential effectiveness have to be estimated on the basis of judgemental predictions. The focus of evaluation turns from specific applications to the capability of an infrastructure to support a range of future activities, and perhaps not to inhibit unforeseen future developments. Evaluation needs to demonstrate the link between the infrastructure investment and subsequent projects whose value to the business can be demonstrated. Such investments are sometimes seen as necessary in order for the company in question to respond rapidly to any moves by competitors. They can be regarded as buying an option on the future profitability of the firm.

A feature of some infrastructure investments, e.g. investing in the introduction of wide-ranging interconnections by means of a corporate network, is that they provide shared facilities whose use develops at different rates and which provide uncertain benefits. There is nothing new in that. The provision of older types of infrastructure – telephones on every desk, many types of administrative services, transport fleets – had very similar characteristics from an evaluation point of view.

Of course many decisions in this category do have more precise targets more appropriate to the second or third rung of the ladder. Thus the decision to introduce office automation may include a precise estimate of the impact of the system on the operations of the typing pool, or the savings possible from avoiding contracting out the printing task by the use of DTP. Nevertheless, infrastructure-type investments are characterized by considerable uncertainty on the kind of impacts the technology will have. More and more of future IT investment is going to fall into this category – the provision of a range of IT capabilities to enable the enterprise to be responsive to market and other pressures.

Sixth rung: Inter-organizational systems

The sixth rung is represented by systems which cross organizational boundaries – systems which are shared by two or more organizations, chiefly trading partners. Although the systems are shared, performing functions for all the collaborating organizations, the value added is not necessarily shared equally by all participants. The most widely discussed inter-organizational systems are electronic data interchange (EDI) systems. There are many examples of EDI systems which have been forced on trading partners by dominant manufacturers as a condition of trading. For the dominated trading partner, e.g. a supplier to a major retail chain, the use of EDI can be classed as a first rung mandatory system. In practice even the dominated collaborator can obtain economic benefits from EDI, though it is the major partner who expects to get most value from the system.

Inter-organizational systems have far-reaching consequences for the partners in that they have a major impact on the relationship between the collaborators. Activities previously carried out by one of the partners may migrate to the other partner with unexpected and important consequences. When American Hospital Supplies (AHS) first put terminals into their customers' offices with a system which permitted the hospital's purchasing officers to interrogate the AHS inventory – and in doing so transferring a significant part of the sales function to the purchaser – they discovered that AHS became the favoured supplier.

For inter-organizational systems, evaluation must involve all partners, even the dominated partners. By joining such systems organizations tie themselves into a standard mode of processing dictated by the joint system. To an extent they lose freedom and flexibility. The focus of evaluation is to balance the loss of total independence against the potential benefits from shared systems, where many of the impacts are difficult to assess.

Seventh rung: Strategic systems

The seventh rung represents the strategic use of IT. Strategic use has been defined by Michael Earl[4] as:

(a) gaining competitive advantage
(b) improving productivity and performance
(c) enabling new ways of managing and organizing
(d) developing new types of business.

In the public sector, where competitive advantage may be less relevant, strategic use is more likely to be concerned with the use of IT to combine the strategic goals of providing improved services to the public, with accountability and management control of the service.

The achievement of strategic use of the technology requires a very close alignment between business strategy and information systems planning. This requires that information systems are seen by senior management to be a strategic resource which must play a role in enabling the business plans to be made effective. Hence the use of IT in this way is characterized by innovation and leadership. But the risks can also be very high. A joint venture by Chemical Bank and AT & T to introduce their home banking product PRONTO had to be abandoned in December 1988 with a write-off of an estimated $70 million in assets. Despite aggressive promotion and technological excellence, PRONTO had attracted only 10 000 subscribers in six years.[5]

A contrasting case from the same industry sector is revealing. First movers may reap very high rewards – witness Merrill-Lynch and its client's cash management system. The firm pioneered the concept of combining a charge card, current account and brokerage service into one product. It breached the traditional boundaries of the banking and securities sectors and, in the event, jumped far ahead of its competitors. Implementation was complex and costly – virtually impossible to justify by the use of conventional methods. Yet its sheer complexity made it difficult to copy and gave Merrill-Lynch a competitive edge. By 1983 Merrill-Lynch had secured a 70% market share.

It is nevertheless true that many of the classic case studies of systems which have been of strategic importance – American Hospital Supplies,

McKesson Economost, the Thomson Holidays TOPS system, and many others – started as rung two or rung three systems, and subsequently proved that they had more than operational significance. Their success at a strategic level was due to the fact that senior management recognized the important advantage the new systems were offering and in a sense realigned the business around them.

More recently companies have proactively sought to align IT plans with business strategy in order to get the kind of advantages the classic case studies have pointed to. In practice there is as yet little evidence that these companies have been more successful in their use of IT to achieve the goals suggested by Earl than companies which have built systems to achieve apparently lesser goals. It may be that the real value of alignment is in avoiding mistaken investments.

Estimating the outcome of investments in strategic IT systems is difficult, but must be attempted.[6] Without some process of evaluation, important opportunities may be missed or champions may persuade managements to take actions which may later prove to be catastrophic. Merely ranking projects in some order of preference is better than relying only on hunch. Conventional cost–benefit and ROI methods are rarely suitable for reaching decisions on strategic investments. Indeed, some of the systems now seen to confer strategic benefits would have failed any test based on cost–benefit and ROI methods. Evaluation based on a broad appreciation of the business situation, and in particular a focus on the competitive situation, coupled with a tight risk analysis, may be the best way to assess whether to invest or not to invest in an application deemed to provide strategic benefit. Perhaps all such projects should show a clear operational benefit, even if such benefits cannot be justified on a purely ROI basis.

Eighth rung; Business transformations

The top rung of the benefits ladder is represented by the applications of IT which enable changes to take place which transform (turn round) an enterprise. Business transformations are always strategic in intent. They are generally forced on an enterprise by lack of economic success, either because of changes in the economic environment to which the enterprise must respond if it is to survive, or because the enterprise has lost its ability to compete successfully.

Good examples of the former are to be found in the American automobile industry. In the 1980s the Japanese automobile industry threatened the survival of the major US manufacturers through the productivity of their manufacturing plants and the quality of their products. One major company saw the problem as one of technology and went a long way, at a cost of nearly $1 billion, to transform its technology. The new plant failed to match the Japanese in productivity or quality. Subsequent diagnosis attempted to understand where they fell short of their global competitors. As a result they decided that transformation must combine changes in technology and changes in management practice, with a strong emphasis on transforming human resource management.[7]

Another major manufacturer went through a similar diagnostic process and as a result drew up a programme of more than 80 separate projects. These ranged from programmes targeted at improving the information flow between design and production engineering and manufacturing, in order to reduce the time taken to bring a new model to the market, to new systems which would enhance the company's relations with its dealer network.

A good example of a company failing to compete is an insurance company which had been market leader but had lost its number one position.[8] For some years management had relied on the company's previous success and failed to appreciate market changes and the rise of competitors. Procedures, e.g. the payment of claims, had not changed for years and had left the company with a poor reputation. A change in senior management was called for. The new management instituted an overall review of management style and practices. It too determined that major transformations were needed. Most of these used IT to support or facilitate the changes.

In all these cases the benefits stem from the transformation as a whole. IT provides only one component of what is often a complex series of changes. It is not possible to attribute a portion of the benefit gained to any one factor. The transformation is enabled by the synergy stemming from all the activities needed to make the transformation work: transformations such as the introduction of JIT in a manufacturing company. JIT involves changes to large parts of the inward logistics of the enterprise. Inventory management, warehousing, purchase ordering, supplier relations, inward distribution and communications all play a part in the transformation. IT is involved in all of these and the effective use of IT is a necessary component of the transformation. But companies have to recognize that successful transformations are rare, and that an organization faced with the need to transform faces some of the most difficult problems that its management has ever had to cope with.

For changes on the top rung of the ladder, the emphasis of evaluation is on the total package, rather than on any one component. For IT the important factors become the choice of the most appropriate technological solutions to enable the major changes to be carried through.

Conclusion

Each rung of the ladder requires a different evaluation emphasis which supports a different set of decision variables. Movement up the ladder changes the emphasis from precise quantification to more judgemental evaluation styles. This does not mean that quantification becomes irrelevant, but that it should be mediated by other techniques such as risk analysis. The involvement of senior management is always important. But the higher the rung the more the projects to be evaluated become issues for the senior management team, and that team must be closely involved in the evaluation and decision-making process. The higher the rung reached, the greater the uncertainty. Hence evaluators need to find ways of reducing uncertainty and decision makers need to be aware of the uncertainties endemic in their decisions.

In the real world there are very few pure cases. Most situations represented by the higher rungs may have components which belong more properly to the lower rungs. The evaluation of such components should be carried out with the emphasis appropriate to that rung of the ladder. For example, a major change programme in an organization may include the establishment of a personnel data base. That data base will be subject to the privacy laws and the component of the system which has to comply with the privacy laws should be treated as a bottom rung application – the emphasis must be on choosing the best way of implementing the relevant conditions.

Chapter 9 has concentrated on the position of a project on the ladder as one of the most important factors to consider in choosing an evaluation method. Chapter 10 goes on to explore the other factors which may influence the choice of method.

Notes and references

1 The best known stages of growth model is probably the one first formulated by Dick Nolan. He suggested, on the basis of some cases, that there was a pattern of IT expenditure which formed an S curve of IT budgets against time. Analysis showed that the curve could be divided into sections and each section had certain characteristics in terms of application types, management style and control of IT expenditure. They saw an organization going through all stages from the earliest to maturity in a sequence of originally 4 and later 7 steps. He introduced the stages model in: Nolan, R. (1973) Managing the computer resource: a stage hypothesis, *Communications of the ACM*, **16**, No. 7, 399–405.
2 Reported in: Nairn, G. (1988) Going for IT, *Informatics*, July, 34–44.
3 The model was first formulated in collaboration with Andersen Consulting; see: Land, F. F. and Lattimer, W. (1991) *Cost-justifying IT Projects – How to Improve the Odds*, unpublished Andersen Consulting Working Paper.

4 Michael Earl has studied the strategic use of IT extensively. He provides a classification of strategic use of IT in: Earl, M. (1987) Information systems strategy formation, in *Criticial Issues in Information Systems Research* (eds R. J. Boland and R. A. Hirschheim), John Wiley and Sons, Chichester, pp. 157–178.

5 *Wall Street Journal,* 5 December, 1988.

6 Eric K. Clemons provides an excellent review of some of the systems in the US which have succeeded in providing their enterprises with strategic advantages: Clemons, E. K. (1991) Evaluating strategic investments in information technology, *Communications of the ACM,* **34**, No. 1, 22–36.

7 Two articles which illustrate the point forcefully are: Osterman, P. (1991) The impact of IT on jobs and skills, in *The Corporation of the 1990s: Information Technology and Organisational Transformation* (ed. M. S. Scott Morton), Oxford University Press, New York and Oxford, pp. 220–243; Walton, R. E. (1991) Organisational change, in *The Corporation of the 1990s: Information Technology and Organisational Transformation* (ed. M. S. Scott Morton), Oxford University Press, New York and Oxford, pp. 244–277.

8 The case is described in: Land, F. F., Detejejaruwat, N. and Smith, C. (1983) Factors affecting social control: the reasons and values, *Systems, Objectives, Solutions,* **3**, Nos 3 and 4, 155–164 (Part I) and 207–226 (Part II).

10 Further factors affecting evaluation

Introduction

Evaluations are needed at different stages in the development of an IT project, and for different purposes. *Ex ante*, organizations wish to decide whether to go ahead with a project. How does this project compare with other IT projects? How does it compare with non-IT projects? Does its internal rate of return exceed the organization's hurdle rate? *Ex post*, organizations wish to know whether a project has been successful. Has it delivered the promised benefits? Is the organization's large and increasing IT expenditure proving worthwhile?

The purpose and timing of the evaluation are just two of the factors that can affect the way it is carried out. As a result the search for a single technique that can deal with all IT investment projects is proving fruitless: the range of circumstances to which that one technique would have to be applied is so wide that no single technique can cope.

This wide range of circumstances comes about because every IT project has characteristics which influence the choice of a suitable evaluation technique. At the same time every evaluation technique has characteristics which point to the set of circumstances in which it could be applied. A first step in evaluation is therefore to understand more about the context in which the evaluation is taking place.

This chapter discusses the factors which define this context. It does this in two stages. The preliminary task is to summarize and bring together some issues already covered which point to the characteristics that differentiate one evaluation from another. This will set the scene for the second stage, which is to integrate these characteristics into a general classification of factors which influence the way in which an evaluation is carried out.

A review of the differentiating characteristics

Chapter 2 described how an organization may want to evaluate (or assess or cost justify or appraise) an IT investment project at any of several stages in its development and implementation. In summary the main stages are when:

1 Strategy is being developed. An IT strategy should be being developed alongside the business strategy and the role of IT will have to be assessed in general terms before either strategy can be finalized. The outcome may be a portfolio of projects, some concerned with specific IT projects and others with the required IT infrastructure.
2 A specific project has been defined. This may be an application or a decision to install IT infrastructure. At this stage the project has usually to be cost justified in the context of other capital investments, and a choice has to be made of the most appropriate design which will meet the requirements defined in the specification.
3 The project is in the developmental stage. Checks must be made to ensure that internal and external changes have not affected the feasibility of the project. At the same time progress on the project has to be assessed to ensure that it is keeping within its budget.
4 The project has reached the point of 'sign-off'. Responsibility is being transferred from the IT department to the user department. The users have to sign that the system does what is required.
5 The project has just been implemented. The system is checked to ensure that it is working as planned and is beginning to deliver the anticipated benefits.
6 The project has been in operation for some time. Evaluation at this stage monitors the project's impact, compares actual costs and benefits with planned costs and benefits, identifies unexpected benefits and costs and records lessons for the future.
7 The project is nearing the end of its life and the feasibility of replacement options is being investigated.

Each evaluation is at a different stage and this can be a particular source of confusion. A recent article[1] reporting on the behaviour of a number of organizations in the US found that organizations are not clear about the different purposes of evaluation and may misunderstand these stages.

Chapter 3 described the range of benefits that can accrue from a project, grouping them into five broad classes:

- Strategic
- Management
- Operational: efficiency and effectiveness
- Technostructure/functionality
- Support.

These imply much more than a list of benefits. They relate to the impact of an IT project on an organization: where, when and how the effects are felt.

Chapter 5 presented a series of case studies which showed that the question of evaluation was bound up with a much wider set of issues. The value of the evaluation process, and indeed the success or failure of the whole project, seems to be embedded in the whole organization: its people, culture, decision-making processes, governance and many other influences. Once the project was thrown into the melting pot, these ingredients inevitably directed its course through the evaluation process and beyond.

Chapter 6 followed up by placing a wide theoretical framework around these case-study-based observations.

Chapter 4 described our own research investigation into the current practice of evaluation and this provides the final element allowing us to classify the factors which influence the way an IT investment decision is handled.

A categorization of the factors affecting project evaluation

The factors affecting the evaluation of an IT project can be classified into five main groups:

- The role of the evaluation.
- The decision environment in which evaluation will take place.
- The system characteristics.
- The organization characteristics.
- The specificity with which cause and effect between an investment and its benefits can be linked.

These five influencing factors will now be described in more detail.

The role of evaluation

The role of an evaluation is defined by the time and level of the organization at which it is carried out.

The point in a project at which a justification or evaluation is carried out has a bearing on the method used. Quite simply, there are different questions to be answered at each stage. To demonstrate this a truncated life-cycle model is shown in the first column of Table 10.1. The second column summarizes the process, or task, which is being carried through at the life-cycle stage and the third shows the approaches to evaluation that might be successful.

Thus, at the very early stages the main concerns are broad, defining high-level goals, sketching the constraints and often within the province of senior management. Boundary values, as a method, is very broad, not requiring detailed numbers, and indicates roughly the comparative

Table 10.1 The effect of the timing dimension

Stage	Process/task	Approach
Strategy formulation	Define goals and constraints; set priorities	Top down; exploratory; high level; involves senior stakeholders
Requirements	Elucidate requirements; gain consensus; enumerate and classify benefits	Top down and bottom up; involves all stakeholders
Specification	Design to meet requirements; develop alternatives; enumerate and classify costs; check benefits	Choose from alternative designs; involves experts
Ex post evaluation	Check on success of implementation; learn from experience; determine follow-up	Measure outcomes; involves all stakeholders

standing of the project or projects. It is therefore worth considering as a candidate method in this situation. For different reasons, MOMC methods need to be considered at the very early stages, in order, for example, to gain high-level consensus.

Whereas at earlier stages management is most concerned with defining the scope of the strategy, and evaluation methods should help in defining that scope, at later stages the concerns are more detailed, involving exact specifications of what the project is intended to do. At the later stages the problem is much more one of measurement, of defining the precise impact of the system in terms of both costs to be incurred, developmental as well as operational, and the benefits which are expected to accrue from the use of the system. Boundary values, for example, are not suitable at the more detailed levels of requirements and specification, whereas cost–benefit analysis might be.

The question of level of evaluation is more straightforward. At senior levels within the organization the issues are wide, e.g. defining strategic goals, sketching the constraints. At lower levels the concerns are more detailed, e.g. the quantification of benefits.

The decision environment

The environment in which a decision has to be made may be more or less constrained. IT decisions do not occur in a vacuum, and the choice of a method of justification must, at the very least, match the culture of the organization. The prior history of implementing information systems has a strong influence.[2] Where there is a proven record of success in the use of IT, management is more likely to accept the estimates of the IT group and to be satisfied with the assurances of 'champions'. But a history of doubtful applications or failure is likely to make management much tougher about investment decisions, and require a tighter appraisal process.

The evaluation may have to conform to an existing corporate procedure, or there may be no established practice. The decision makers may expect only hard quantified benefits to be considered, or they may be happy to deal with soft qualitative benefits. The cost of the evaluation procedure may also be an issue, as may the availability of staff trained in the use of a method.

Table 10.2 The effect of the environment dimension

Characteristic	Sub-characteristic	Approach
Goal-driven	'Mission-related'	Broad comparison of all projects
	Detailed/direct	Demonstrate that project meets goals; compare costs
Constraints	Competitive; imposed; legal	Check functionality; compare costs
	Locked into supplier	Check functionality; demonstrate profitability
	Financial hurdles	Show hurdles are overcome
Decision process	Standard	Follow process
	Ad hoc	
Benefits	Quantitative	
	Qualitative	

In Table 10.2 the characteristics of the environment are shown, broken down into a more detailed set of (sub) characteristics (i.e. of goal, constraint or decision process) and approach. For example, the situation may be goal-driven, either in the general sense that all projects must be justified back to an existing 'mission', or in the particular sense that the project has to meet pre-specified goals (or both). In the former case a specific project needs to be justified in the context of a broad comparison of all projects; in the latter it is necessary first to demonstrate that a project will meet the pre-specified goals and that it compares favourably with others in terms of cost. These considerations prompt two further questions about the method of justification: first, are detailed precise numbers required or will a broad picture suffice; second, is there a trade-off to be made between the cost of the procedure and the value added by it?

The system underlying the IT investment

This can be described by two variables. The first variable is the nature of the system: whether it is a specific application or provides an infrastructure. The second variable is the relationship of the system to the business: whether the system is in a supporting role (e.g. financial, documentation) or core (at the heart of the company's production and delivery chain).

The criteria by which a system should be judged must reflect the nature and the purposes of that system. An evaluation method must therefore include, or provide a means for establishing, these criteria. For example, if a system investment is made for strategic purposes, to increase revenue, then the system must be evaluated using a method which includes increased revenue as a criterion for evaluation. If it does not, or if there is no means of identifying an increase in revenue as attributable to the system, the method is not valid.

Table 10.3 shows the nature of the system, the relationship to the business and the purpose of the system.

Table 10.3 The effect of the system dimension

Nature of system	Relation to business	Purpose of system
Application	Core	Strategic
Infrastructure	Support	Informational
		Transactional

The organization making the investment

The competitive position of the organization may also affect evaluation. One factor is the industry situation: whether it is stable or whether there is, or is forecast, a lot of change; restructuring, turbulence and high levels of IT development. A stable situation suggests that reliable data may be available and points to a technique which operates on detailed information: ROI methods, for example. An unstable situation suggests that reliable data may not be available and consequently an exploratory technique such as simulation may be preferable.

The second factor is the leadership role of the organization: whether it aims to pioneer or to follow. In a leadership role the evaluation is likely to be exploratory and need to give results fast. In a follower role there will be existing investments by other organizations which will provide a guide to the decision makers. A technique such as boundary values may be used to indicate appropriate levels of expenditure.

Cause and effect relationships

The degree to which it is possible to predict the impact of the new system is an important factor in determining how to do an evaluation.[3] The impact of the new system may be direct – putting in a payroll system will directly reduce the cost of calculating pay and producing payslips. The costs and benefits are likely to be measurable and an accounting-based method can be employed.

But a system designed to provide a manager with 'better' information in order to improve decision-making depends upon the capability of the manager to use the better information to deliver the expected benefit. The impact is indirect and a technique that handles an unknown range of possibly intangible benefits, such as MOMC, will be more suitable.

The degree of uncertainty is equally important. In a well-defined area the impact of a system may be clear. For example, the analyst may be able to make a precise calculation of the number of staff saved by putting in a computer-based sales order system. But the computation of the likelihood of reduced stockouts from a new inventory control system is far less certain. Again, uncertainty will point to a technique which is better at dealing with it, probably one based on exploration as opposed to accounting calculations.

Conclusions

The organization wishing to sharpen its IT investment decision-making must first recognize that there are evaluation techniques other than discounted cash flow methods such as ROI. It must then try to find which technique is most suitable for its IT investment.

Each of the available techniques is applicable to a particular set of circumstances. The task for the organization is to characterize the circumstances in which the IT investment is to be evaluated, using the above five dimensions as a guide, and then to search through the evaluation techniques to find one which most closely matches the investment.

This matching process is no more than an *ad hoc* method based on a detailed study of investments and techniques. However, such a lengthy approach may not always be possible and will in any case be subjective. What is really needed is a systematic means for matching investment and technique.

This is the subject of the next chapter. It is important to pursue the question of matching very carefully because the process of evaluation can be just as important as the outcome: evaluation creates awareness and understanding of the investment and this may prevent later implementation problems.

Notes and references

1 Kumar, K. (1990) Post implementation evaluation of computer-based IS: current practice, *Communications of the ACM,* **33**, No. 2, 203–212.
2 Reilly, R. R. and Schreck, E. M. (1990) *Perspectives for Justifying Investments in Information Executives*, Working Paper.
3 Kydd, C. T. (1989) Understanding the information content in MIS management tools, *MIS Quarterly,* **13** (3), 277–290.

11 Matching an IT investment with an appropriate evaluation method

Previous chapters have provided the information which should make it possible to decide which evaluation method is suitable for a particular IT project. Chapters 7 and 8 described a range of evaluation methods and their characteristics; Chapter 10 described the factors to do with an IT investment which influence its evaluation. In theory at least, all this information should make it possible to match an IT investment with a suitable evaluation technique but the process would be both lengthy and imprecise. The purpose of this chapter is to find a *systematic* means of performing the matching process.

Chapters 7 and 8 outlined the principles of the most important methods of cost justification and project evaluation. Table 8.1 summarizes these techniques and their characteristics.

These different characteristics give each method a different 'profile'. For example, in a cost–benefit analysis, numbers are more important than process; the results may feed into a further decision process such as ROI; costs and benefits which are external to the organization, such as those which might accrue to customers, are included; and the method seeks a cost-effective solution. By contrast, MOMC methods focus attention on the process by which preferences are derived and incorporated into a decision. It follows that different methods will be applicable to different situations. Chapters 7 and 8 therefore provided one side of the matching 'equation'.

In Chapter 10 the other side of the equation, the description of the situation in which a method is potentially to be used, was provided. In that chapter the factors which influence the way evaluation of a project is carried out were classified into five main groups:

- the role of the evaluation
- the decision environment in which evaluation will take place
- the system characteristics
- the organization characteristics
- the specificity with which cause and effect between an investment and its benefits can be linked.

The matching process

The process has three stages:

1 Represent the circumstances of the project which is to be evaluated as points on a series of 2 × 2 matrices (based on Chapter 10).
2 Use the information about evaluation techniques to locate each technique at some point on a 2 × 2 matrix (based on Chapters 7 and 8).
3 Overlay the matrices to match project with technique.

The process will be illustrated by applying it to a fictional 'package tour operator', an organization which puts together 'holiday packages' comprising travel and accommodation. It is the intermediary between travel agents and airlines, car hirers, hotel owners etc. The project is the installation of a large system which links the tour operator with on one side travel agent's offices located throughout the country and on the other side with airlines, hotels etc. The system means that a customer and his or her travel agent can get immediate information on availability, prices, alternatives, etc., and immediate confirmation.

In this example the evaluation is taking place at an early stage in the development of the project: when the first decision to go ahead is being made, and before the details of the system have been specified.

Stage 1 Representing the project

The circumstances in which an investment is to be evaluated have the five broad dimensions described in the previous chapter.

The role of evaluation

The role of an evaluation is defined by two subdimensions: the time and level at which it is carried out.

At an early stage (up to the requirements stage) management is still trying to develop strategy, and evaluation methods should help in defining its scope. At a later stage (from the specification stage forwards) the project or programme is being defined. The concerns are more detailed, involving exact stipulations of the project's purposes. Here the concern is much more one of measurement, of assessing the impact of the project in terms of detailed costs and the benefits.

The question of level of evaluation is more straightforward. At higher levels within the organization (strategic) the issues are wide, e.g. defining strategic goals, sketching the constraints. At lower levels (tactical) the concerns are more detailed, e.g. the quantification of benefits.

This dimension can be represented as a 2 × 2 matrix (Figure 11.1).

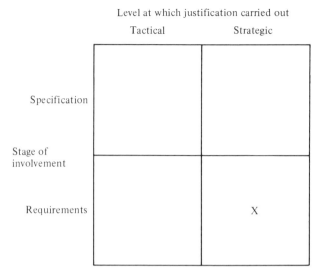

Figure 11.1 Timing and level

For a particular project these characteristics can be summarized by placing a cross in the appropriate quadrant. Both vertical and horizontal variables are either/or (rather than, for example, on a scale from 1 to 10) and so the cross is placed in the middle of a quadrant.

For example, in the case of the original justification of the tour operator's system, the evaluation is taking place at the strategic level and at the requirements stage. A cross would be placed in the middle of the bottom right quadrant, as shown.

The decision environment

IT decisions are not made in isolation, and the choice of an evaluation method must match aspects of the decision environment such as, for example, the culture of the organization. It must conform to existing corporate appraisal procedures, or if there is no established practice, it must be able to adapt to imported or *ad hoc* methods. The decision makers may expect only hard quantified benefits to be considered, or they may be accustomed to handle a wider range of benefits. The cost of the evaluation procedure may also be an issue.

This dimension has four subdimensions:

1 The decision process – whether it is standard for all projects or *ad hoc*.
2 The type of benefits the project is expected to bring – whether they are hard and easily quantifiable or soft and qualitative.

3 The importance of numbers – whether or not an attempt has to be made to attach numbers to all benefits and costs.
4 The cost of the justification technique – whether simple (cheap) methods only can be used or whether sophisticated (expensive) ones are acceptable.

This dimension can be represented by two 2 × 2 matrices (Figures 11.2 and 11.3).

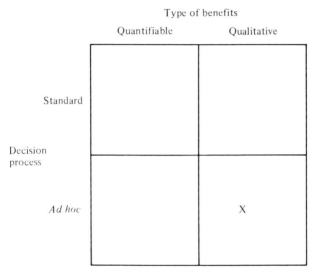

Figure 11.2 Benefits and decision process

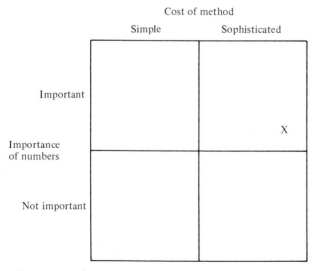

Figure 11.3 Cost of method and importance of numbers

Again, for a particular project this characteristic can be summarized by placing a cross in the appropriate quadrant. However, in this case three of the four subdimensions can be scaled. For example, the importance of numbers can be assessed at some point on a range, perhaps on a 1 to 10 scale. The cross might therefore be placed anywhere in the matrix rather than in the middle of a quadrant. The exception is the decision process: whether it is standard or *ad hoc*. This is a yes/no variable.

For example, in the case of the tour operator's system, the subdimensions might be assessed as below:

1 Decision process: *ad hoc*

2 Type of benefits:

Quantifiable   Qualitative

——————————————————————————————————x————————————

1   2   3   4   5   6   7   8   9   10

3 Importance of numbers:

Important   Not important

——————————————————————x————————————————————————

1   2   3   4   5   6   7   8   9   10

4 Cost of method:

Simple   Sophisticated

——x————————

1   2   3   4   5   6   7   8   9   10

These assessments mean that crosses would be placed in the matrices as shown in Figures 11.2 and 11.3.

The system underlying the IT investment

This can be described along two subdimensions.

The first is the purpose of the system. At one extreme it may be a specific application, such as inventory control, and at the other it may provide an infrastructure on which a range of applications could run.

The second is the connection between the system and the business: the system may be in a supporting role (e.g. accounting, personnel, documentation) or core (at the heart of the company's value chain).

As with other dimensions, the criteria by which a system should be judged must reflect the nature and the purposes of that system. An evaluation method must therefore include, or provide a means for establishing, these criteria. For example, if a system investment is made for strategic purposes, to increase revenue, then the system must be evaluated using a method which includes increased revenue as a criterion for evaluation.

The two subdimensions can be represented by a 2 × 2 matrix (Figure 11.4).

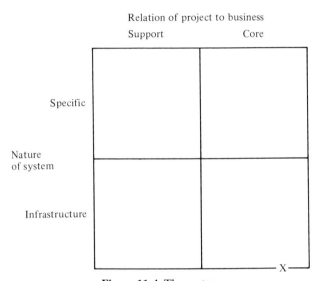

Figure 11.4 The system

Both subdimensions can be assessed on a scale. For example, in the case of the tour operator's system, the subdimensions might be assessed as below:

1 Nature of system:

Specific application   Infrastructure

1   2   3   4   5   6   7   8   9   10

2 Relation of project to business:

Support   Core

1   2   3   4   5   6   7   8   9   10

A cross is then placed on the matrix as shown in Figure 11.4.

The organization making the investment

The competitive position of the organization may also affect evaluation.

The first subdimension is the industry situation: stable or turbulent. A stable situation suggests that dependable data may be available and suggests a method which operates on such detailed information. An unstable situation suggests a lack of good data and therefore that an exploratory method may be preferable.

The second subdimension is the leadership role of the organization within the industry: a pioneer or a follower. In a leadership role the evaluation is likely to be exploratory, giving fast results. In a follower role there will be existing investments by other organizations to guide decision makers and provide data.

Organization characteristics are described by a 2 × 2 matrix (Figure 11.5).

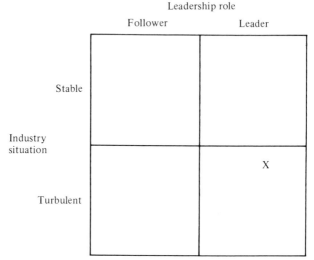

Figure 11.5 Organization characteristics

In the case of the tour operator's system, the subdimensions might be assessed as below:

1 Industry situation:

Stable   Turbulent
────────────────────────────x──────────────────────────
   1   2   3   4   5   6   7   8   9   10

2 Leadership role:

Follower   Leader
──────────────────────────────────────x──────────
   1   2   3   4   5   6   7   8   9   10

A cross is then placed on the matrix as shown in Figure 11.5.

Cause and effect relationships

The impact of the new system may be almost completely predictable or totally uncertain. This dimension can be split into two subdimensions.

The first is the directness of the impact. If the impact is direct the system has an immediate first-order effect. An example is a payroll system where the system acts to replace manpower and thereby to reduce these and other costs. However, a system intended to provide a manager with 'better' information in order to improve decision-making does not have a first-order effect. It depends upon the capability of the manager to use the better information to deliver the expected benefit. This impact is indirect.

The second variable is the uncertainty of the impact. In a well-defined area the impact of a system may be clear. For example, the analyst may be able to make a precise calculation of the number of staff saved by putting in a computer-based sales order system. But the computation of the likelihood of reduced stockouts from a new inventory control system is far less certain. As before, the degree of uncertainty will point to an evaluation method which is better at dealing with it, probably one based on exploration as opposed to accounting calculations.

Cause and effect relationships can be described by a 2 × 2 matrix (Figure 11.6).

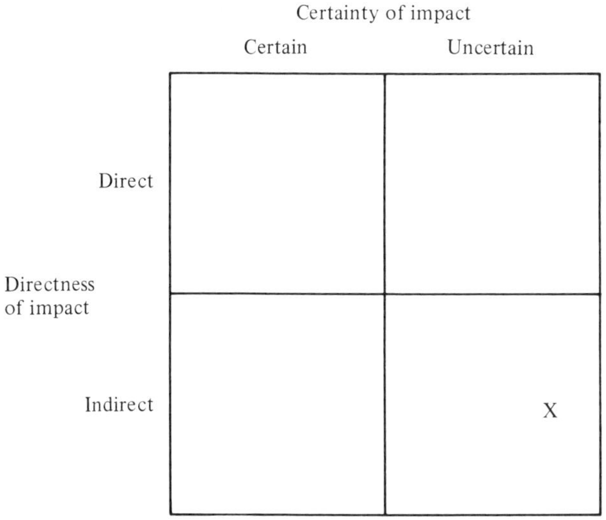

Figure 11.6 Cause and effect relationship

In the case of the tour operator's system, the subdimensions might be assessed as below:

1 Directness of impact: a yes/no situation. In this case the impact is indirect, depending upon the usage of the system by travel agents and related travel organizations.

2 Certainty of impact:

Certain   Uncertain

---X---------

  1   2   3   4   5   6   7   8   9   10

A cross is then placed on the matrix as shown in Figure 11.6.

The five matrices describing the circumstances of the evaluation are then overlaid to provide one overall summary matrix (Figure 11.7).

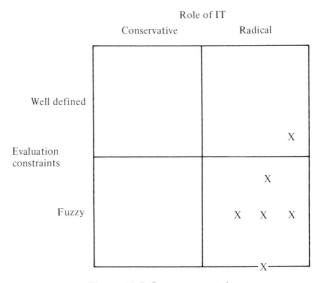

Figure 11.7 Summary matrix

The horizontal scale of the summary matrix (Figure 11.7) combines the subdimensions shown in Figures 11.1 to 11.6:

1 Level of evaluation
2 Type of benefits
3 Sophistication of evaluation methods used
4 Relationship of project to business
5 Leadership role of organization
6 Certainty of impact

Without suggesting that this is a precise definition it can be said that the horizontal scale summarizes the *role of IT within the organization*: conservative or radical.

The vertical scale of the summary matrix also combines the subdimensions shown in Figures 11.1 to 11.6.

1 Timing of evaluation
2 Nature of decision process
3 Importance of numbers
4 Nature of system
5 Industry situation
6 Directness of impact

Again without attempting a precise definition, the horizontal scale summarizes the constraints on *decision-making* and *evaluation*, both inside and outside the organization: well defined or fuzzy.

Stage 2 Locating the evaluation methods

The circumstances in which evaluation is to be carried out have been described along several *situation dimensions* and, after overlaying, by a 2 × 2 summary matrix (Figure 11.7).

The evaluation methods described in Chapters 7 and 8 also have *characteristics* which make them most suitable for use in particular sets of circumstances. Comparing the situation dimensions with the characteristics of the evaluation methods suggests that the methods can be allocated to the quadrants of the 2 × 2 matrix as shown in Figure 11.8:

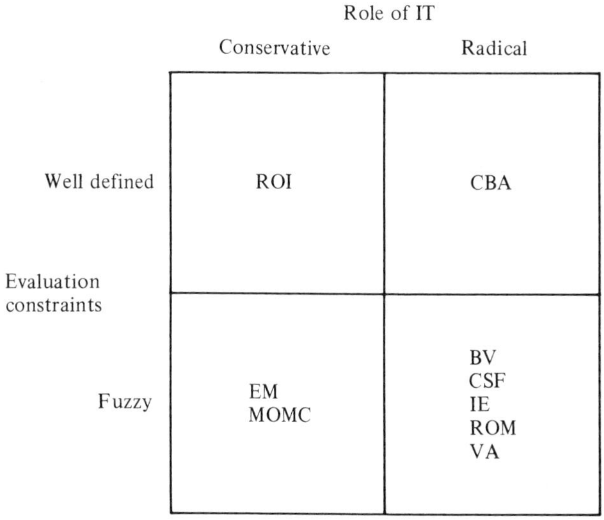

Figure 11.8 The evaluation methods. BV, boundary values; CBA, cost–benefit analysis; CSF, critical success factors; EM, experimental methods; IE, information economics; MOMC, multi-objective, multi-criteria; ROI, return on investment; ROM, return on management; VA, value analysis

- *Top-left quadrant.* ROI is located in this quadrant. It is a well-established accounting method and there is long experience of its use when IT is being applied in traditional efficiency-seeking projects in well-defined circumstances.
- *Top-right quadrant.* Cost–benefit analysis, like ROI, is applied in well-defined circumstances. Unlike ROI it has the capability to deal with a wide range of benefits. It should be located in the top-right quadrant.
- *Bottom-left quadrant.* In this quadrant IT is being applied in conservative ways but in a fuzzy decision-making environment. Experimental methods and MOMC methods are exploratory in nature. They can cope with uncertainty in the decision-making process and, especially, they have some capacity to bring consensus and commitment to stakeholders.
- *Bottom-right quadrant.* This quadrant is probably the most difficult. IT is being applied in radical ways in a fuzzy decision-making environment. Evaluation methods will have to deal with systems which have a wide range of benefits and which are probably large, going right across the organization, and outside it. The methods allocated to this quadrant are able to handle large projects with substantial organizational impacts.

Stage 3 Matching

The locations of the crosses, whether clustered or dispersed, are used to suggest the range of techniques that might be applied. In some cases all crosses may fall within the same quadrant, giving a strong indication of exactly which techniques might be suitable. In other cases the crosses might be spread around, indicating that the choice is not clear-cut and that several techniques could be used.

In the case of the tour operator's system, the crosses lie mainly in the bottom-right quadrant, indicating that the most suitable techniques are: boundary values, critical success factors, information economics, return on management and value analysis. Return on management would try to capture the wide range of intangible benefits for a system that is at the core of the company's business. In a competitive environment, boundary values would monitor and compare expenditure levels. Critical success factors would ensure the system was linked to the main business issues. Information economics would satisfy the need for quantification. Value analysis would analyse the benefits which, at the time the system was being planned, were far from certain. At the same time the method indicates that the more straightforward techniques such as ROI might not be appropriate.

Conclusions

The organization wishing to sharpen its IT investment decision-making must first recognize that there are evaluation techniques other than discounted cash flow methods such as ROI. It must then try to find which technique is most suitable for its IT investment.

Previous chapters have provided the information necessary for the selection of an evaluation method appropriate for the investment being evaluated. Each of the available techniques is applicable to a particular set of circumstances. The task for the organization is to characterize the circumstances in which the IT investment is to be evaluated, using the above five dimensions as a guide, and then to search through the evaluation techniques to find one which most closely matches the investment.

This chapter goes a stage further. Its purpose has been to propose a *systematic* means for carrying out the matching. The matrix method is a simple, short procedure for achieving a match and encouraging objectivity. Of course the matching process is by no means precise: in order to make the matching process workable, a trade-off between complexity and practicability had to be made. Nevertheless the process can promote an awareness of the options available and guide managers' thinking.

12 Concluding thoughts

We started our investigation into the evaluation of IT investments with a quotation from the Management in the 90s (MIT90s) research programme:

> Everybody does cost/benefit analysis on projects. Most of them are fictional. The saddest part is that it is not just the benefits that are fictional but the costs are as well. They don't begin to assess what the real costs of the system are. You do cost/benefit analysis to get money.

The strong implication is that current practice in the evaluation of IT investments is a tissue of lies and therefore a waste of time. Is this inevitably the case both now and in the future? If it is, then the previous 11 chapters have been to no avail. Managers are not going to follow the 'right' method of evaluation if the whole concept is flawed because those carrying it out are working from a different, and hidden, agenda on which true evaluation does not feature.

Undeniably the area is packed with contradictions. For example, in one of the case studies we held the role of champion up for admiration and praised the virtues of a particular incumbent. Yet the role of a champion is precisely to go beyond the bounds of duty so that a project is accepted and implemented. What can this mean except that we expect the champion to cheat in order to get the 'go ahead' for a project? And what easier way is there to cheat than by bending the rules of the evaluation process? If we praise the champion we diminish evaluation; if we promote the proper role of evaluation we marginalize the champion.

It is also certainly true that meaningless rituals will be of little value to an organization. Nevertheless, at the worst – the worst meaning a largely fictitious process – evaluation still has some value. However evaluation is carried out, the existence of the project and some of its impacts and implications will be brought to the attention of some of the relevant managers. People will start to think about the project.

At the best – the best meaning an accurate and reliable assessment of the project's total impact – the organization will secure a range of benefits going well outside the main focus of an accurate decision to go ahead. As the case studies show, good evaluation can have a significant bottom line impact.

So, what can be done to move evaluation away from the 'worst' scenario and closer to the 'best'? The key may well lie in the second half of the MIT90s quote:

> We have trouble convincing ourselves of value in business terms. We cost justify new systems on the basis of lies and overstatement, we then don't measure the true business value.

It is sometimes said on current affairs programmes that the reason criminals continue to commit crimes is the small probability of being found out. The same could also be true of evaluation: the reasons people cheat on evaluation is that they won't be found out. As the MIT90s quote suggests, this is because organizations do not in general conduct post-implementation audits. Organizations have no procedures by which unachieved or exaggerated benefits, or suppressed or underestimated costs, can ever see the light of day. Our research, and that of others, supports the view that carefully executed post-implementation audits of IT investments are great rarities.

Why are organizations so unwilling to carry out post-implementation audits of IT investments? It is not necessarily that they lack the capabilities and resources to correct the faults that have led to failure. The problem is not even that organizations do not know what has caused failure. The first problem is often that it is not known, except at an anecdotal level, whether the outcome of an IT investment has been a success or failure.

The argument in favour of auditing IT investments seems clear but excuses are always made: 'it's too expensive', 'it's too late', 'the guilty have left the company' etc. Our prediction is that this will not and cannot continue. As chief executives become more concerned about the value for money they are getting from rapidly increasing IT expenditures and rapidly expanding IT departments, and as a few organizations venture along the path of IT audits and get surprising results, so the concept will become part of regular and essential business practice. Perhaps IT audits will become as common as accounting audits. In the new 'information age' it is not a question of 'if' but 'when'.

However, the quest for better evaluation should be two-pronged. The first prong stems from the acceptance of audits; the second from an improved ability to carry out evaluations. The previous 11 chapters have been aimed at the latter. The point is that once the concept of regular post-implementation audits is established, the lessons our research pointed to and which we have highlighted in this book will take on a further significance.

Our research looked at 16 major IT investments, ostensibly to vet the way they were appraised prior to the decision to go ahead being taken. In the course of the research we found that the issue could not be isolated; it had implications which were rooted in all aspects of the organizations' business and management processes and resources. The 'further significance' of evaluation lies in this wide-ranging influence.

The research pointed to lessons which were not at all obvious at first sight. Organizations and managers should:

- *Face their opportunities squarely.* If an IT project has strategic potential, the evaluation process should not hide the potential away behind a barrier of (sometimes fictional) efficiency benefits which are more acceptable to the formal decision-making process. Otherwise the big benefits might wither through lack of attention.
- *Make mental models explicit.* Behind evaluation and decision-making processes there can be hidden a series of implicit assumptions which differ from one organization to another, from one function to another and from one stakeholder to another. They must be brought into the open.
- *Use evaluation to learn.* Evaluating a project educates stakeholders – about the project, about their fellow stakeholders, about IT and about the business itself and what its objectives are. These are significant yet underrated benefits.
- *Understand that evaluation is about horses for courses.* Unlike many other capital expenditures, IT investments cannot be handled through a single comprehensive technique. It simply does not exist, nor is it likely to.

The need for evaluation, and its problems, is not new. Our last quotation comes from an eminent source a long time ago:

> Business systems, like other facts of life, are largely governed by tradition, prejudice and habit . . . and can only be brought under a rule of reason based on careful analysis of concrete facts.[1]

We can be fairly certain that the issue will be with us for some time yet.

Notes and references

1 Taken from the *Harvard Business Review*, Vol. 1, 1923, and quoted by Graeme Norris of the Centre for Information Economics at a Unicom Conference on 29 January 1992.

Index